P9-EDC-249

CROSSROADS: 1913

CROSSROADS: 1913

by
Paul M. Angle

RAND McNALLY & COMPANY
Chicago • New York • San Francisco

First Printing April 1963
Library of Congress Catalog Card Number: 63:11146
Printed in the United States of America
by Rand McNally & Company

The roads diverge at the point where we stand

The New Freedom (1913)
Woodrow Wilson

FOREWORD

I HAVE long believed that the years between 1898 and 1914 were the golden age of the American people. Quick victory in the Spanish-American War not only made the United States a world power, but also forced the European nations to recognize that fact. A dawning century lifted spirits and offered the promise of unlimited progress. The rapid development of the automobile, the proliferation of telephones, the increasing use of electricity, and the invention of the airplane seemed to confirm the promise. Life was comfortable, and while people worked long hours, they worked under little tension. Peace prevailed, and as the years passed the belief grew that the world had seen the last big war.

My conviction as to the idyllic character of this period has been buttressed by a duty that I have enjoyed for eighteen years. In compiling a section, "Fifty Years Ago," for *Chicago History*, the quarterly publication of the Chicago Historical Society, I have scanned every page of the *Chicago Tribune*, then as now a national newspaper, from 1895 through 1913. No one can do this without recognizing that the United States was no paradise in the first decade of the century. Many people barely subsisted on the wages they received. Impure milk and water brought on frequent epidemics. Physicians were almost helpless when confronted by diseases then common: typhoid fever, scarlet fever, and pneumonia. Nevertheless, on balance, at least for the average man or woman, the years were good.

Then, in August, 1914, war broke out between the great European powers. Overnight, the world changed. So it seemed at the time; so it seems to many today. I am not so sure. As far as the United States was concerned, I believe that 1913 was the year of transition, the year when one era came to an end, the year when a new era began.

Consider, if you will, the income tax, and the changes, social and economic, which it effected. Consider the New Freedom with its shift of emphasis in the goals of government. Consider the coming of age of the automobile and the evidence it offered of the perfection of mass production. Consider the beginnings of automation, bearing then the lowly term of labor saving. Consider the acceleration of the suffrage and prohibition movements. Consider the revolution in women's dress and the increasing frankness in drama and fiction. And consider the impact of "modern" art and "modern" music. I hold that after 1913 life in the United States would have changed radically even if there had been no World War.

Therefore this book. In it I have not attempted a scholarly study. I have not probed deeply for causes nor have I assessed results. Except in a few instances I have refrained from comparisons, trusting the reader to make his own. I have tried to picture developments as they unfolded before the eyes of mature, intelligent, inquisitive people of the time. For this reason I have adopted the chronological approach. That technique has drawbacks—namely, the division of some topics into several sections and overlapping in the treatment of others—yet it seems to me to be more realistic than grouping a variety of subjects into neat, unrelated compartments.

In this book my primary reliance has been on contemporary reporting. The *Chicago Tribune* has been a primary source, but I have supplemented it with many other newspapers, most of which I have named in the text. Magazines have been invaluable, particularly *The Independent, The Nation,* the *Literary Digest, The Outlook,* the *Century Magazine, Life, The Theatre,* and the *Ladies Home Journal.* Two great biographies saved me an enormous amount of spade work: Arthur S. Link's *The New Freedom,* Vol. II in *Wilson* (Princeton University Press, 1947-1960); and Ray Stannard Baker's *President, 1913-1914,* Vol. IV in *Woodrow Wilson, Life and Letters* (Doubleday, Doran, 1927-1939). *The American Year Book, 1913* (Appleton, 1914); and *The World Almanac, 1914,* were only less helpful. I also put to good use Julius Mattfeld's *Variety Music Cavalcade, 1620-1950* (Prentice-Hall, 1952); *Spalding's Official Baseball Guide for 1914;* Selig Perlman and Philip Taft, *History of Labor in the United States,* Vol. IV in John R. Commons' larger work with the same title (Macmillan, 1918-1935); and *The Days of Armageddon, 1909-1919,* Vol. VII in Elting E. Morison's edition of *The Letters of Theodore Roosevelt* (Harvard University Press, 1951).

Every author incurs personal obligations which he can never begin to satisfy by merely mentioning those who have helped him. My indebtedness is particularly heavy to Miss Alma Skinner of Washington, D.C., who has repeatedly tapped the resources of the Library of Congress for my benefit; to Miss Paula Angle, my daughter, who has assembled many of the photographs which I have used as illustrations; and to the following members of the staff of the Chicago Historical Society, who unreservedly placed their knowledge and skills at my disposal: Mrs. Paul Rhymer, custodian of prints and photographs; Miss Margaret Scriven, librarian; Walter Krutz, photographer; and Miss Margery Melgaard, typist extraordinary. The staffs of the Newberry Library and the Harper Memorial Library, University of Chicago, have been, as always, most helpful.

Paul M. Angle
Chicago Historical Society

January 25, 1963

CONTENTS

Winter: The Opening Round

Spring

Summer

CONTENTS

Autumn

Winter: The Closing Round

Epilogue

LIST OF PHOTOGRAPHS

Front Section:

CROSSROADS: 1913

West Point Cadets arriving at the inauguration
Wilson takes the oath of office
Wilson and Taft after the inauguration
Could eight dollars a week keep a woman virtuous?
J. P. Morgan, with Mrs. Morgan
Wreckage left by the Omaha tornado
An Omaha street, after the tornado
Peru, Indiana, under water
Downtown Dayton under water
Dayton, Ohio, after the flood receded
Wilson about to break a precedent
John T. McCutcheon on presidential messages

Back Section:

Bryan bringing everlasting peace
One view of the new dances
Her husband might have liked it
Ragtime: an American export to Great Britain
For the man who wanted to be in style, and could afford it
For the man who wanted to be in high style, and could afford it
Sears Roebuck styles in men's suits
The shoes that women wore
Proper dresses in the eyes of the President's daughters
Some women had other ideas
The bikini of 1913
U.S.S. Texas. Two of these a year, or one, or none?
Confederate veterans arriving at Gettysburg for the reunion
Union and Confederate veterans at Gettysburg
Theodore Roosevelt, still the idol of millions
Jess Willard, heavyweight "white hope"
Jack Johnson, heavyweight champion of the world
Bryan before a Chautauqua audience
Something could be said for the income tax
City traffic, Michigan Avenue, Chicago
City traffic, State Street, Chicago
Rival managers, McGraw and Mack at world series

List of Photographs

CROSSROADS: 1913

WINTER

The opening round

Early in the evening of December 31, 1912, in dry and pleasant winter weather, crowds began to gather in New York's parks and public places. Many boys who had brought horns and other noisemakers found themselves out of favor and subsided. As eleven o'clock approached, Times Square, Herald Square, Madison Square, Union Square, and City Hall Park were jammed.

In Herald Square a great screen had been placed on the south façade of the Herald Building. In front of the screen a choir of 500 voices sat expectantly. On the stroke of eleven, five bagpipers rose before the choir, and for half an hour stirred the huge mass of people—50,000 was the estimate—with the patriotic music of various nations.

At 11:30 the choir rose. "Mine eyes have seen the glory of the coming of the Lord" carried to the limits of the crowd. The words of "The Battle Hymn of the Republic" flashed on the screen. The audience joined in. Next came "O God, Our Help in Ages Past," and "Nearer My God to Thee." Three cornets sounded "Taps." As the last clear note floated on the silence—the awesome silence of a huge mass of people—the pipers gave out the opening notes of

"America." Fifty thousand voices sang the four stanzas.

The New Year's Eve Committee had provided for one minute of silence before midnight. As the minute hand of the Herald clock reached 11:59, quiet settled over the Square. On the stroke of 12:00 a great shout went up. Cheers lasted for some minutes, and then the people who had taken part in the celebration drifted away to their homes. The same program was followed at the other public meetings.

In the hotels and cafes a different mood prevailed. Every dining room was filled to capacity. Diners, adorned with paper caps, tossed toy balloons and confetti and pounded miniature drums. At midnight, following long-established local custom, lights dimmed, orchestras played dirges. The lights came back and the music took on life to greet old Father Time accompanied by the New Year, usually personified by little girls who danced between the tables and sometimes on them. Corks popped with abandon.

An employees' strike at the Waldorf-Astoria did not prevent the hotel from accommodating 3,000 celebrants. The McAlpin, with dining rooms "gorgeously decorated," took care of 1,500. The staid Plaza crowded in 1,800 and distributed eighty musicians among its five dining rooms. Names known to readers of society pages over the country appeared in the various guest lists: Mr. and Mrs. Patrick A. Valentine, Mr. and Mrs. Frank J. Gould, Frank L. Schoonmaker, Hamilton Fish, C. K. G. Billings, Elihu B. Root—and many more.

"It was a noticeable feature," the *New York Herald* commented, "that the diners represented citizens from every state in the Union, and from nearly every country in the world. New York represented not only the Metropolis of America, but also the New Year's festivities of the entire country."

But to represent is not to monopolize. Boston staged its first public celebration of the advent of the New Year, an event which, aided by clear weather no colder than many a day in September, drew 75,000 to the Common. At 10:30 the Municipal band began its concert with a march. Then the musicians swung into "Marching Through Georgia." The crowd took up the tune. With "Tenting Tonight on the Old Camp Ground," "Dixie," and "Columbia, the Gem of the Ocean" the audience took over completely, and the band could be heard only by those who surrounded the bandstand.

The program changed. A cornetist played "The Rosary" as a solo; a baritone rendered "When the Midnight Choo-Choo Leaves for Alabam'." The audience yelled for more, and Mayor Fitzgerald, known fondly as "Honey Fitz"[1] saw that they got what they wanted. Standing in front of the band he sang the verses and led the audience in the chorus of one popular song after another. With "Sweet Adeline" he reached peak performance. All sang at the top of their lungs. At the conclusion of the song the *Boston Globe* commented ambiguously: "He got all the applause that was coming to him."

In hotels and restaurants Boston celebrated in much the New York pattern, except that most of those who held reservations attended the theater first. Therefore the rush

[1] *Grandfather of President John Fitzgerald Kennedy. The* Chicago Daily News, *November 5, 1962, published an Associated Press news photograph captioned: "A Campaigning Baritone—Edward M. (Ted) Kennedy sings "Sweet Adeline" for the audience at an Irish dance in Boston during windup of campaign for the Senate seat from Massachusetts."*

to the places of resort did not take place until 10:30, when Boylston Street from the Tremont to the Copley-Plaza suddenly filled with gorgeously gowned women and their escorts in evening clothes.

Each of the big hotels and restaurants followed the same program. Orchestras played, quartets sang, and costly souvenirs were distributed to all the revelers. A few minutes before midnight most of the lights were extinguished. On the stroke of 12:00 the figures "1913" flashed on screens or in arrangements of electric lights. The diners threw confetti and paper serpentines, tooted horns, and blew shrill whistles. And, as in New York, corks popped incessantly.

The New Year moved across the country. In Chicago, word had spread that the police would wink at the 1:00 A.M. closing hour. Saloons, cafes, and hotels had laid in enormous supplies of wines and liquors and hired extra bartenders, "and thus," in the words of the local *Northwestern Christian Advocate,* "the devil had set his house in order to entertain harlots, panders, bums, lecherous rich, innocent boys, and pure girls—all whirling in the same caldron of iniquitous indulgence."

The same paper offered its readers a lurid account of the evening:

"As the hours sped on and the old year was about to close, the multitude and tumult surged in careless, drunken currents of humanity. . . . When the hour of twelve struck, pandemonium reigned. The crowds burst over into the streets, girls were swept along in the surging multitude and subjected to indignities that were not resented because of the hour. Young men by the scores marched staggeringly in the beginnings of fast-approaching drunkenness. The burlesque houses were receiving and discharging their crowds as rapidly as possible to accommodate those impatiently waiting. All along the streets, and chiefly near the hotels and cafes, the abandon was so pronounced one could easily imagine he detected in the composite roar of voices in revelry the laughter of Satan himself. Who knows?"

Other accounts, presumably more objective, agree that the city indulged in the wildest celebration in many years. But the clubs gave quiet entertainments, and 5,000 people attended a musicale at the Art Institute.

In New Orleans celebrants jammed streets so thick with fog that the lights gleamed feebly in nimbi of yellow haze, but the half-mist, ever threatening rain, failed to dampen the general ardor. Along Canal Street crowds pushed, jostled, tugged, shouted, blew horns, and rang cowbells whenever they found elbow room. Carnival organizations in costume paraded the streets. Hundreds of automobiles, each carrying its burden of boisterous occupants, tried to circle the congested center of the city. When the New Year came in, their horns joined with the whistles of river boats tied up at the levee to create unprecedented pandemonium.

Two hours later, San Francisco ushered in the New Year in what the *Examiner* described as a "blazing carnival of turbulent gaiety." According to the paper's reporters, the entire population of the city had spilled into the streets, restaurants, and hotels. By eight o'clock the sidewalks were crowded; by nine they were black. In Fillmore Street and in the Mission high carnival prevailed. Chinatown welcomed an alien New Year with illuminations and firecrackers. But Market Street, from Eighth Street to Montgomery, was the center of raucous gaiety. There the crowds threw confetti and clanged bells with greater abandon than in any other part of the city. There almost everyone wore little Turkish fezzes lettered with such sentiments as "Ah there, Kiddo," and "I Don't Care If I Do." A stream of automobiles, each loaded with surging, laughing humanity, pushed slowly up and down the thoroughfare.

The hotels and restaurants offered much the same kind of entertainment as similar establishments in other parts of the country, although it is doubtful that any hotel in the country matched the St. Francis in providing "Hawaiian dancers, brass bands, clown bands, barnstormers and yodel singers" for its 1,500 patrons.

The nation's newspapers, reporting the New Year's festivities, usually noted in a line or two that most of the churches held watch services. They attempted no count, but it could be possible that far more people attended these quiet ceremonies than congregated in the noisy hotels and cafes of the big cities.

And for a certainty, the vast majority of the people of the United States treated New Year's Eve as any other day, going to bed at their accustomed hour, and rising the following morning hardly aware that 1912 had become 1913.

New Year's Day—January 1, 1913—was marked, in Washington, by the most brilliant presidential reception in many years. On an afternoon that seemed to be a belated bit of Indian summer, 8,000 people streamed into the White House to offer their good wishes to the retiring President, William Howard Taft, and the First Lady of the land. Every member of the Cabinet and their wives stood in line to greet callers who ranged in rank from M. Jean Adrien Antoine Jules Jusserand, Ambassador of France, who, in the absence of Baron Hengelmüller of Austro-Hungary, was dean of the diplomatic corps; General Leonard Wood of the United States Army; and seventy-six-year-old Admiral George Dewey, hero of Manila Bay; to ordinary citizens moved by simple curiosity.

Over the country newspaper readers could feel a pang of sympathy for the big, jovial, well-intentioned President who had somehow failed to measure up to the expectations of his countrymen. They could only laugh at the reported New Year's resolutions of elder statesmen. "Uncle Joe" Cannon, tyrannical Speaker of the House of Representatives about to go out of office as a result of the Republican debacle of 1912, told an inquirer:

"Some good brother might think that the best resolution one can make is never to take another drink or to smoke another good cigar, and never to look at a pretty woman, while another man might think, like our good German brothers, that a stein of beer is made to be drunk, a pretty girl to be loved, and a good cigar to be smoked.

"My set of resolutions for the New Year is that I won't smoke more than one cigar at a time and I won't drink more than is good for me. As to the girls—well, at my time of life ["Uncle Joe" was 77] I don't suppose it is necessary for me to make any resolutions about fair women."

Senator James E. Martine of New Jersey, sixty-three years of age, declared that he intended to "lead a decent life and vote the Democratic ticket, take aboard liquor in reasonable quantities, enjoy good health and pleasant surroundings and leave every man free to lead his life and vote as he jolly well pleases."

Senator Knute Nelson of Minnesota, seventy years old, made only one resolution: to search until he found a good brand of chewing tobacco. "I've been obliged," he explained, "to change the brand I've been using because they put it up in tins and let the quality deteriorate. I want something more progressive."

The nation that in these various ways moved into 1913 consisted, for the first New Year in its history, of forty-eight states. (New Mexico had not been admitted until January, 1912; the door had been opened to Arizona on February 14.) Total population aggregated 95,000,000 or thereabouts. Within the country people were moving and relocating with a velocity that upset old balances almost annually. By 1910 the Federal census takers found that the Pacific states—California, Oregon, Washington—had become the fastest growing section of the nation, showing an increase of 73 per cent in a single decade. Hard on their heels came the mountain states, including New Mexico and Arizona, which grew by 57 per cent in the same period, but with far fewer inhabitants involved. At the other end of the scale stood what the Census Bureau designated as the East South Central states—Kentucky, Tennessee, Alabama, and Mississippi—which showed a growth of only 11 per cent between 1900 and 1910.

Despite the rapid growth of the Pacific states, California stood no higher than twelfth place in 1913. New York retained the first place which it had held for a century, followed in order by Pennsylvania, Illinois, and Ohio.

The census figures revealed that the cities of the country were growing like hothouse plants. Between 1900 and 1910 New York jumped from 3,437,000 inhabitants to 4,767,000; Chicago, in the same decade, from 1,700,000 to 2,185,000. Behind these two metropolitan giants ranged eight others, each counting populations of more than 400,000:

Philadelphia	1,550,000
St. Louis	687,000
Boston	671,000
Cleveland	561,000
Baltimore	558,000
Pittsburgh	534,000
Detroit	466,000
Buffalo	424,000

Yet the country remained predominantly rural, with more than half of the people living on farms or in towns with fewer than 2,500 inhabitants. But the analysts of the 1910 figures reported a significant trend: in the first ten years of the century the urban population had increased by 34 per cent, the rural population by only 11 per cent.

The United States, it was clear, would, before long, become an urban nation.[1]

On the evening of January 11 the members of Chicago's Commercial Club, their starched white shirt fronts resplendent, gathered at the Blackstone Hotel. The three hundred diners included the leading bankers, merchants, executives, and professional men of the city. The importance of the occasion was indicated by the presence at the head table of Mayor Harrison, Governor Deneen, and Governor-elect Dunne. Woodrow Wilson was scheduled to make his first public address since his election.

The President-elect knew that few of the men he faced favored the policies for which he stood. That fact did not prevent him from making a bold statement of his purposes. First of all, he asserted, the natural resources of the coun-

---

[1] *The census of 1960 gave the fifty states of the Union a population of 179,000,000. The Pacific states, now comprising Alaska and Hawaii as well as Washington, Oregon, and California, continued to be the fastest growing section of the country, increasing by 40 per cent from 1950 to 1960. The Mountain states followed, growing by 35 per cent in the same period. As in 1910, the East South Central states made the smallest gain, only 5 per cent.*

In 1960 New York and Pennsylvania still held first and second rank among the states, but California had jumped to third place; Illinois and Ohio had dropped to fourth and fifth.

In 1960 the ten largest cities were:

New York	*7,782,000*	*Baltimore*	*939,000*
Chicago	*3,550,000*	*Houston*	*938,000*
Los Angeles	*2,479,000*	*Cleveland*	*876,000*
Philadelphia	*2,203,000*	*Washington*	*764,000*
Detroit	*1,670,000*	*St. Louis*	*750,000*

try must be conserved and administered for the common benefit. The raw materials of industry must be available to everyone on equal terms. Wilson reminded his audience that the people—"I mean the rank and file of our people"—did not believe that all men were "upon an equality in their access to the resources of the country." Businessmen, specifically, were under widespread suspicion. "That is unjust to you," he said. "It is unjust to everybody with whom business deals and everybody whom business touches."

The audience applauded warmly. These were good words to hear from a man whom many of those present considered a dangerous enemy.

Credit, the speaker continued, must also be at the disposal of everyone on equal terms. "I am not entering into an indictment against the banking methods of this country," he asserted. "The banking system of this country does not need to be indicted. It is convicted." That there were inner and outer circles of credit—"regions of chilly exclusion and regions of warm inclusion"—everyone knew. This situation had to be changed.

Boston, with 697,000, had dropped to thirteenth place; Pittsburgh, with 604,000, to sixteenth; and Buffalo, with 533,000, to twentieth.

Metropolitan areas offer a more realistic ranking. In 1960 the ten largest metropolitan areas were:

New York	*15,400,000*
Los Angeles	*6,570,000*
Chicago	*6,520,000*
Philadelphia	*3,970,000*
Detroit	*3,840,000*
San Francisco	*3,275,000*
Boston	*2,910,000*
Cleveland	*2,090,000*
Washington	*2,050,000*
St. Louis	*2,050,000*

By the 1960 count the rural population, still defined as people living on farms or in towns with fewer than 2,500 inhabitants, stood at 54,000,000, or 30 per cent of the whole. 125,269,000, or 70 per cent, were classified as urban.

Again there was applause. If some of the bankers frowned, there were plenty of men present who resented and distrusted the concentration of capital in the East.

The President-elect broached another topic. "We must see to it that the business of the United States is set absolutely free of every feature of monopoly." He paused. "I notice you do not applaud that," he resumed. "I am somewhat disappointed, because unless you feel that way the thing is not going to happen except by duress, the worst way in which to bring anything about."

He had no intimate knowledge of the processes of business, the speaker confessed. Therefore he had to consult with men who possessed that knowledge, and how could he rely on their advice unless he knew they believed in the same ends he believed in?

So far Wilson had spoken conversationally, almost casually. Now, in his urgent desire to convince, his voice became vibrant.

"I have made promises which I regard as intimately involved with my essential honor. I serve only one master and no group of individuals can speak for my master.

"I am a trustee for the prosperity of the United States in council and the council that is not common council, the council that does not include you, is imperfect council, is council which will mislead.

"Won't you come in? Have you not come in? Is it not your purpose to re-establish economic freedom in the United States? Aren't we all in the same boat? Can't I enlist you tonight in the common enterprise? There is no bright prospect otherwise."

Many in the audience—an audience as skeptical, if not hostile, as Wilson would face in years—were deeply impressed. Harold F. McCormick, Vice-President of the International Harvester Company, called the address a masterpiece. On the other hand a number of influential newspapers dissented. Both the *New York Times* and the *New York Evening Post,* which had supported Wilson in the presidential campaign, were sharply critical. "Where," the *Times* asked, "did our President-elect get the facts on which he bases the ideas which he is repeating in words and in print? . . . Looking ahead there can only be embarrassment and misadventure in pandering to error, or in legislating to remedy evils which do not exist outside of muckrakers' romances." The *Post* attributed prevailing "uneasiness" in financial circles to concern over the ideas which Wilson had expressed, and fear that extremely delicate problems would be handled clumsily. The stock market dropped.

Reaction over the country, however, was well represented by *The Outlook,* which carried the name of Theodore Roosevelt as a contributing editor. "Mr. Wilson . . . has discovered . . . that the office to which he has been chosen is, among other things, a pulpit. No congregation is any the worse for the fact that the preacher talks plainly about moral conditions and points plainly the way for an improvement in moral purpose and spirit. . . . As a member of the President-elect's congregation *The Outlook* is glad that he has preached this sermon."

A few days after his Commercial Club speech, the President-elect gave further evidence of his independence and, perhaps, his puritanical spirit. He asked the chairman of the inauguration committee to dispense with the inaugural ball, a fixture since the days of Franklin Pierce. He considered it a needless expense and a function no longer necessary for the entertainment of visitors. Wives of Congressmen and prominent Democratic politicians hastily countermanded orders for ball gowns; Washington merchants winced. The *Chicago Tribune* surmised that he was influenced by apprehension that at least some of those who would attend the ball could not be prevented from indulging in the "Turkey Trot," "Grizzly Bear," or the "Bunny Hug," deplored by all the arbiters of taste and morals.

The country at large, cared little. As the editor of *The Nation* put it:

"To declaim against bosses, even to wage unrelenting war upon them, is comparatively easy; but to lay hands upon a social custom—what is this but to trifle with fate? Every four years, since a time whereof the memory of man runneth not to the contrary, the citizens of Washington have enjoyed the privilege of paying five or ten dollars for admission to the Pension building . . . and of seeing, for a fleeting moment, the President and his wife as they appeared upon the balcony for a look at the dancing throng. Every four years the merchants of the District have spent, or rather invested, thousands of dollars in preparations for the inauguration, relying upon the proceeds of the inaugural ball for reimbursement. Upon all this Mr. Wilson has frowned. The arrangement does not strike him as befitting the dignity of an inauguration, and he makes bold to hint as much. Outside of Washington at least, there will be many to agree with him."

Madison Square Garden had become a crystal palace. Mirrors—more than a mile of them—lined the walls. A huge canopy of dark blue cloth gave the effect of open night. Although the "sky" was set with 7,000 lights, crystal chandeliers furnished additional illumination.

Blocks away in Grand Central Palace the decorator had worked with an equally extravagant hand. The result, an observer commented, "smacked of such widely separated periods as those of Versailles and the California missions with a dash of the Doric thrown in," but even so, the effect was "pleasing."

No setting could be too lavish for the million dollars' worth of pleasure motorcars, motorcycles, accessories and parts exhibited in New York's thirteenth annual Automobile Show. At the first show, held in the Garden in 1900, twenty cars had been displayed. When the doors of both the great halls were opened on January 11, 1913, visitors could have counted more than 700 vehicles, the product of eighty-eight makers. A one-passenger roadster could be had for as little as $395, but a certified check for $7,000 had to be tendered if one coveted a finely finished, enclosed, six-cylinder limousine.

Observers spotted trends. Lines were longer, more graceful, "stream-lined," as a new term had it. An increasing number of cars, though still a minority, had left-hand drives. Electric lights had become universal: dealers admitted that without them a car couldn't be sold. And the electric self-starter, introduced two years earlier, was fast becoming a standard feature. At least 50 per cent of the cars at the show were equipped with the device. "It is the marked feature of the season," a *New York Times* reporter asserted, "and means the banishment of the backbreaking crank into a limbo nearly as complete as that which holds the wheezy 'one lunged' horseless carriage of a dozen years ago."

By 1913 the automobile industry had become the marvel of the American economy. The number of passenger cars registered had increased from 8,000 in 1900 to 1,190,000. Of this total nearly half—461,500—were produced in 1913 alone. The record proved, said the *World Almanac,* "that the motor car has entirely passed the stage where it can be classed as a luxury and that it is today regarded as quite as much of a necessity by the man of moderate means as was the horse a few years ago."

Experts in 1913 noted that buyers were indicating a preference for a lighter car with economy of operation and upkeep. They all meant the Ford Model T, though none would mention it by name. This sturdy, economical little car which, in the words of Charles E. Sorensen, one of its developers, "anyone could afford to buy, which anyone could drive anywhere, and which almost anyone could keep in repair," was sweeping the country. Introduced on October 1, 1908, it caught on so fast that the Ford factory, recognized as the most efficient in the industry, could not keep up with the demand.

But the fertile brains of Henry Ford and several of his engineers were working on production methods that would surpass in speed and economy anything the world had seen. The assembly line was nothing new—Ford had been using it for years in the production of such components as motors, magnetos, and carburetors. But when all the components were ready they had to be brought together at the chassis and put in place. The new Ford plan was a continuous assembly line in which the chassis would move along and receive each component part at the right time. The operation was perfected in 1913. The results were startling. In 1912 the best Ford record for stationary chassis assembly had been 728 minutes of one man's work; by the end of 1913 that time had been cut to 93 minutes. Ford production jumped from 78,440 Model T's in 1911–12 to 168,304 in 1912–13 to 248,307 in 1913–14.

Simultaneously, Ford reduced prices, cutting the runabout from $525 at the beginning of 1913 to $500 at the end of the year, the touring car from $600 to $550. Small wonder that the company was producing 96 per cent of the passenger cars in the low-priced field—$600 or less—and two-fifths of the industry's total output.

The commercial branch of the automobile industry lagged far behind passenger car production, yet it too was growing. In 1913, 23,500 trucks were manufactured, bringing the total registration to 67,667. Most of those in use were gasoline powered, rather than electric, of 1,000 to 1,500 pound capacity, and costing from $1,875 to $2,400.

In spite of the substantial gain made in 1913, the experts differed about the future. One, writing for the *World Almanac,* asserted that "there is nothing to indicate that this branch of the industry will ever progress as has the passenger car division." Upkeep costs were excessive, and must be drastically reduced before "the motor-propelled business vehicle will begin to cut seriously into the field of the horse." *The American Year Book's* automobile specialist held the same opinion. The manufacturer, he claimed, too often produced vehicles unsuited to the work they had to do; just as often the user did not know what he needed.

And "bad driving, fast driving, and resulting high cost of upkeep" created a further handicap.

On the other hand, *The Outlook* predicted that it would not be many years before there would be more trucks than pleasure cars in operation. "The horse and wagon have just about as much chance of successfully competing with the motor truck as the stagecoach had with the locomotive." The editor quoted Thomas A. Edison, admired as the country's most reliable oracle, on the future of the electric car: "Probably the greatest future field for the electric car is in commercial transportation. It is rapidly doing away with the horse. The chief reasons for the enormous jump forward the electric has recently taken are its low operating cost and its extreme reliability. . . . The electric is the car of the future."

The experts might have found a portent in Chicago's experience. On February 9, 1913, the *Tribune* reported that the city hauled more than 5,000,000 tons of merchandise by motor in the past year. "Auto wagons" numbered 2,600; each traveled between 35 and 40 miles a day. Marshall Field and Company, with 109 trucks, claimed the biggest fleet. Altogether, the motor-driven vehicles were doing the work of 12,000 horses. "Highly imaginative men," the reporter concluded, "have indulged themselves with fanciful expectations of the horseless city."

In the production and use of automobiles the United States led the world. In aeronautics she ranked last by every standard of measurement. In July, 1913, there were

193 licensed airplane pilots in the country. France counted 968; Great Britain, 376; Germany, 335. Of planes of all kinds either in service or on order, the United States had exactly 75, compared with 550 in France, 375 in Germany, and 315 in Russia.

In military aviation it was the same story. Between 1908 and 1912 the United States appropriated a total of $255,-000 for military aviation; in 1913, $125,000. In the same year France appropriated $7,400,000; Germany, $5,000,-000; Russia, $5,000,000; and Great Britain, $3,000,000. Even Mexico outdid the Colossus of the North with an appropriation of $400,000.

Significantly, the five pages (3,500 words) on aeronautics in the *American Year Book* for 1913 are devoted almost entirely to foreign activities and developments. Not a single one of the twenty-two official airplane records listed there was credited to an American flyer or an American plane.

No event of the year 1913 better illustrated the transition between one era and another than the wedding, on January 22, of Helen Miller Gould and Finley J. Shepard.

The bride, daughter of Jay Gould, financier and railroad manipulator who left a fortune estimated at $25,-000,000 on his death in 1892, represented the moneyed aristocracy of the United States. In certain respects his daughter's wedding followed the pattern established by her class. The ceremony was held at Lyndhurst, the family country estate at Tarrytown, New York, where under a blue sky lawns green even in winter sloped down to the sparkling Hudson. Royalty attended—the Duke and Duchess of Talleyrand (the bride's sister) and their three-year-old son, the Duke of Sagan. The servants were present (forty in number) from the town house as well as from Lyndhurst, and neither of the principals thought it strange that the superintendent of the cow barns should attend in his rough corduroy trousers and coarse tan boots, with his worn and faded felt hat crushed in one hand. In the manorial tradition Tarrytown and nearby Irvington declared a holiday. The gates of the Gould estate were thrown open and the townspeople allowed to wander as they pleased. Hundreds crowded close enough to the house to hear the music that preceded and followed the ceremony.

But there were new departures. Miss Gould, approaching forty-four years of age, had announced, to the consternation of fashionable modistes on Fifth Avenue, that her trousseau would cost less than $1,000. She had limited the guest list to 100, including the servants. And the curious people of the neighborhood who explored the grounds saw strange structures: the public sewing school into which she had converted her father's bowling alleys, a building for a school of cooking and domestic science even then under construction where dog kennels had stood.

Throughout her mature life this daughter of a man called cold, unscrupulous, and selfish had devoted much of her wealth to philanthropy. She had given a library building and The Hall of Fame to New York University. During the Spanish-American War she had donated $100,000 to the United States Government and had herself nursed sick and convalescent soldiers. Army and Navy Y.M.C.A.'s and the Railroad Y.M.C.A. had been subjects of continuing benefactions.

(Many of the wedding gifts displayed at Lyndhurst were sent in the name of the officers and men of various army posts or ships of the navy. From the Railroad Y.M.C.A. of the western lines came a jewel box and a clock, the former a miniature reproduction of Jay Gould's private railway car, the latter a small model of the Railroad Y.M.C.A. building at St. Louis, a gift to the bride in memory of her father.)

That night a thousand down-and-outers at the Bowery Mission in New York City enjoyed a "wedding dinner" provided by the bride—a hearty meal of roast beef, turnips, potatoes, bread, pie, and coffee. And when the food ran out, the police used their night sticks on the hungry hundreds who had come too late for the feast.

James Francis Thorpe—Jim Thorpe—was born in 1888 in Indian Territory, now Oklahoma, of Irish, French, and American Indian ancestry. He attended the Haskell Institute at Lawrence, Kansas, and went from there to the Carlisle Indian School at Carlisle, Pennsylvania. He starred on the football team in 1908, and was then sent south for two years for further conditioning. Back at Carlisle in 1911, his play then and in 1912 won him a place on the All-American teams for both years.

In the summer of 1912 Thorpe had gone to Stockholm as a member of the American Olympic Team. There he had won both the pentathlon (200 meter dash, 1,500 meter run, broad jump, discus, and javelin) and the decathlon (100 meter dash, 400 meter run, 1,500 meter run, 110 meter hurdles, high jump, shot put, discus, pole vault, broad jump, and javelin), a double victory without precedent and, fifty years later, still unmatched.

The Olympic Games were open only to amateurs. In the third week of January, 1913, a Worcester, Massachusetts, newspaper charged that Thorpe, while in the South in 1909 and 1910, had played professional baseball and therefore had been ineligible to represent the United States on the 1912 Olympic Team. At first the Indian denied the allegation, but on January 26, while the governing board of the Amateur Athletic Union was considering his case, he made his confession. From Carlisle he sent a pathetic letter:

"I played baseball at Rocky Mount and at Fayetteville, N. C., in the summer of 1909 and 1910 under my own name. . . . I never realized until now what a big mistake I made by keeping it a secret about my ball playing, and I am sorry I did so. I hope I will be partly excused by the fact that I was simply an Indian schoolboy and did not know all about such things. In fact, I did not know that I was doing wrong, because I was doing what I knew several other college men had done, except that they did not use their own names."

Thorpe returned all the trophies he had won since 1908 to be awarded to the runners-up in the events in which he had participated.

Headlines of the time referred to the Indian as the "World's Greatest Athlete." As late as 1950 an Associated Press poll accorded him the same accolade.

One week after Thorpe's confession he signed a contract

with the New York Giants at a reputed salary of $7,500, close to the top for a baseball player at that time.

On the same day, Ban Johnson, president of the American League, awarded Bill Dineen, umpire, $200 as a prize for handling games with the minimum waste of time. Dineen's games had averaged 1 hour and 55 minutes in 1912.

The Independent (February 6, 1913) represented a strong body of opinion when it printed an editorial attacking Henry Bacon's classic design for the Lincoln Memorial to be erected in Washington. "How Lincoln Would Have Laughed!" the caption read. "Why should the Great Liberator be commemorated by an edifice characteristic of a people [the Greeks] whose wisest men upheld the institution of slavery as natural, indispensable and eternal?"

What do they think of this in Lincoln's own country, the Middle West? The editorial cited a recent protest by the Illinois Chapter of the American Institute of Architects to the effect that the design had nothing in common with the race that it should inspire or with the man it was intended to honor. On the contrary, it would declare "the architectural poverty and sterility of America in assuming the necessity of our imitation of the classic style."

But what do they know about art out in Illinois?

So President Taft had signed the Bacon bill and $2,000,000 would be spent in erecting a marble monument "that will represent to posterity all too faithfully the architectural ideals of America in the twentieth century."

(It was ironic that Henry Bacon should have been born at Watseka, Illinois, while his father, a civil engineer, was employed by the Illinois Central Railroad; that he had attended the University of Illinois for a year; and that he had not only worked on the plans for several of the World's Columbian Exposition buildings but also had spent considerable time in supervising their construction. —But 1913 was not 1893.)

Shortly before his inauguration Woodrow Wilson remarked to a friend: "It would be the irony of fate if my administration had to deal chiefly with foreign affairs." That he would at least become concerned with foreign affairs became apparent shortly before he took office.

February 9, 1913, witnessed a violent eruption in Mexico.

Two years earlier the dictator Porfirio Díaz, eighty years old and senile, had been forced to abdicate. Francisco Madero, author of a book highly critical of the Díaz regime, *La Succesión presidencial en 1910,* emerged as the national leader. In October, 1911, Madero was elected president. It was soon apparent that the situation called for qualities which the tiny (five feet two inches), mild-mannered man with the squeaky voice did not possess. He was too weak to restrain his friends, too humane to assassinate his enemies. Mexico soon suffered from an administration as corrupt as that of Díaz.

Counterrevolutionary movements coalesced. One was led by General Bernardo Reyes, who was apprehended and, instead of being executed in the Mexican tradition, was imprisoned at Tacubaya, a suburb of Mexico City. On February 9, 1913, the local garrison revolted. With Reyes at their head, the soldiers marched on the National Palace. There loyal troops sprayed them with machine-gun fire, killing Reyes, many of his followers, and some 200 innocent men, women, and children on their way to Mass at the nearby cathedral. Madero, frightened, put General Victoriano Huerta, a murderous drunkard but a good soldier, in command of the Palace guard.

For the next ten days Huerta and Félix Díaz, nephew of the old dictator and leader of another counterrevolutionary movement, showered the city with gunfire, never, unfortunately, hitting each other, but killing hundreds of peaceful inhabitants. On February 18 Henry Lane Wilson, U. S. Ambassador, brought the two opponents together at the American Embassy where they agreed to join forces and take over Mexico from Madero's faltering hands. "A wicked despotism has fallen," Wilson reported to the State Department at Washington. Four days later Madero and Vice-President Pino Suárez were killed "while attempting to escape."

With thousands of American nationals living in Mexico and millions of dollars invested there, the United States could not ignore these developments. On February 12 President Taft took the extraordinary step of calling the Cabinet to meet at midnight. As a result three more battleships were ordered to the squadron already assembled off Veracruz. Four days later, after another prolonged meeting of the Cabinet, presidental secretary Charles D. Hilles announced: "Various dispatches from Mexico were considered and it was decided that the information so far received afforded no basis for a change in the policy of the government of the United States, already indicated many times in the last two years."

The administration sent 3,000 Marines to the coast of Cuba to be held in readiness for action in Mexico and strengthened Army posts along the border. But President Taft had made up his mind to do nothing. On February 22, the day of Madero's assassination, before a dinner of the American Peace and Arbitration League, he said:

"Mexico for two years has presented a sad picture to every lover of his kind, to every supporter of popular government, to every man hopeful of establishing peace under a stable government.

"But we must not despair. We must not, in a case like Mexico—for it differs from the Central American republics—take such action as shall give them to believe that we are moved by selfish purposes, or arouse them to opposition to us.

"We must avoid in every way that which is called intervention, and use all the patience possible, with the prayers that some power may arise there to bring about peace throughout that great country."

With these words of high resolution he bequeathed a major headache to his successor.

"All heaven is shouting and the devil is glum!"

With this declaration Billy Sunday summed up the results of his revival campaign in Columbus, Ohio.

The evangelist had reason to be jubilant. Although he

had been conducting revival meetings for sixteen years, he had had little success in large cities. A campaign in Spokane, Washington, in 1909, had not aroused the people, nor had another in Toledo in 1911. The Columbus revival was a final attempt. If it failed, he would limit himself to the smaller cities, where he could "convert" 20 per cent of the population instead of only 4 or 5 per cent, his record in Spokane and Toledo.

The Columbus revival, beginning in late December, 1912, and lasting seven weeks, was a smashing success. It set records: the largest attendance, the largest number of converts, the largest sum raised for the evangelist. Between 750,000 and 1,000,000 people attended ninety-five tabernacle meetings. More than 18,000 persons, a good 10 per cent of the city's inhabitants, signed cards of intention. The sum of $18,590 was raised for expenses; $21,000 for Sunday himself. According to the *Ohio State Journal:*

"For more than seven weeks hundreds of business men had neglected their private affairs, for an equal period social engagements were disregarded or side-tracked; for that length of time sixty churches had closed their doors, their pastors had devoted the bulk of their time to advancing the work of the campaign, and during all those days, Rev. Billy Sunday—the baseball evangelist—had talked and prayed, sweated and pranced about the platform, besought and entreated with sinners, flayed with scalding invective every sort of wickedness, and endeared himself personally to multitudes who either had been openly or covertly antagonistic.

"Under the spell of his oratory and the persuasive influence of his co-workers, all manner of men were made to take a new view of life. City and county officials, saloonkeepers and professors, society women and shop girls, school children and avowed agnostics, stood up and said, 'I publicly accept Jesus Christ as my personal Savior.' "

The success of the Columbus revival made Sunday a figure of widespread controversy. His sensationalism offended many. Goliath was an "old stiff who strutted up and down blowing about his height and his bravery." Along came David to "call his bluff." The young man "socked the giant in the coco between the lamps, took his sword, chopped off his block, and the gang skiddooed."

His theology, if it could be called that, was primitive; his methods crude. A writer in *The Congregationalist* recalled an incident of the Toledo revival. One of Sunday's ministerial supporters, disturbed by a sermon about evolutionists, remonstrated with him privately. The next day, from the platform, Sunday singled out his critic, shook his fist at him, and shouted: "Stand up there, you bastard evolutionist! Stand up with the atheists and the infidels and the whoremongers and the adulterers and go to hell!"

One who had attended many of the Columbus revival meetings could find little religion in the performance. "Good music," he wrote, "a splendid organization, a howling mountebank to call in the crowd, an usher to every six seats, a personal worker to every three make it easier to go forward than to go out into the open air. I do not think that any discerning intelligence can justify giving this man the sanction of the approval of any religious organization."

Billy Sunday, his critics said, was making a business of evangelism and fast becoming a rich man. The $21,000 which he took personally from the Columbus meetings would pay the salary of the average minister for twenty years; Sunday's income for twelve months would support a hundred foreign missionaries. The evangelist was his own best apologist. On his last day in Columbus he defended his methods in characteristic language:

"You must be willing to do things in a different way to move the unconverted toward salvation, to sacrifice your own personal prejudices for the sake of the folks on the outside. . . . If I were a pastor of a church I'd have a brass band in front of the church every Sunday night to let the devil know there's something doing down there.

"There's a verse in Scriptures on 'Feed my lambs'; but in some instances it ought to read, 'Feed my giraffes,' because some folks put the fodder so high that nobody can reach it.

"I never aspired to be a heady, throaty, intellectual preacher. I am satisfied to put the gospel in such a way that the foundryman at the fires and the toiler in the ditch will understand it and be led to repentance. I don't care three whoops this side of perdition whether any gang in this town likes it or not."

Where, the *New York Times* had asked of Wilson's Commercial Club address, had he got his facts about the "Money Trust"? The editor should have known the answer: from the well-publicized hearings of the Pujo Committee.

In February, 1912, the House of Representatives had directed its Committee on Banking and Currency to ascertain whether an overpowering concentration of financial and banking power existed in the United States. The job was assigned to a subcommittee headed by Arsène Paulin Pujo, of Louisiana. On February 28, 1913, the committee published its findings in the form of a majority report, a minority report, and a brief by J. P. Morgan and Company. The majority report held that there was "a great and rapidly growing concentration of the control of money and credit in the hands of a few men," that the domination that was available for financing large security issues and for stock exchange loans was "at least as effective as . . . the control of the United States Steel Corporation over the steel industry," and that this control was "fraught with peril to the welfare of the country."

The inner circle of the "Money Trust," the majority found, consisted of J. P. Morgan and Company, George F. Baker and the First National Bank of New York, and James Stillman and the National City Bank—institutions which together controlled resources of $1,300,000,000. In close alliance were Lee, Higginson and Company; Kidder, Peabody and Company of Boston, and their allied banks; Kuhn, Loeb and Company with their foreign connections; and the three largest banks of Chicago, The First National, The Illinois Trust and Savings, and the Continental and Commercial, with combined resources of $561,000,000.

The resources of these institutions endowed them with power; interlocking directorates enabled them to exercise it. The committee found that the partners of J. P. Morgan and Company and the directors of the two great New York banks held 341 directorships in 112 corporations in the fields of finance, insurance, transportation, manufacturing, and public utilities, and that these corporations had resources of more than $22,000,000,000.

"It would, of course, be absurd to suggest," the report

read, "that control of the bulk of the widely distributed wealth of a great nation can be corralled by any set of men. . . . It is not, however, necessary that a group of men shall directly control the small savings in the banks or the scattered resources of the country in order to monopolize the great financial transactions or to be able to dictate the credits that shall be extended or withheld from the more important and conspicuous business enterprises. This is substantially what has been accomplished. . . . The powerful grip of these gentlemen is upon the throttle that controls the wheels of credit, and upon their signal those wheels will turn or stop. . . . This inner group and allies thus have no competition, either from others or among themselves, for these security issues, and are accordingly free to exact their own terms in most cases."

The Morgan brief denied the existence and even the possibility of a "Money Trust." That there were evils "neither few nor trifling" was admitted, but these were attributable to "a clumsy and outworn banking system rather than to the schemes of men." Such concentration of financing as existed, principally in New York, Boston, and Chicago, had come about because great banks were necessary to finance great enterprises, and the great banks were to be found in these centers.

The brief made a plea for the rectitude and high principles of the bankers:

"Your counsel asked more than one witness whether the present power held by bankers in this country would not be a menace if it lay in evil hands. Such an inquiry answers itself. All power, physical, intellectual, financial, or political, is dangerous in evil hands. If Congress were to fall into evil hands the results might be deplorable. But to us it seems as little likely that the citizens of this country will fill Congress with rascals as it is that they will entrust the leadership of their business and financial affairs to a set of clever rogues. The only genuine power which an individual, or a group of individuals, can gain is that arising from the confidence reposed in him or them by the community."

The facts brought to light by the Pujo investigation were irrefutable. Their significance might be questioned, but intelligent opinion the country over accepted the report as proof that the banking and currency system of the country was badly in need of thorough reform.

"No such hubbub had been raised in many years, no such chatter about the province of art."

With this crisp statement David Lloyd, art editor of the *New York Evening Post,* evaluated, quite accurately, the first international exhibition of modern art presented under the auspices of the newly formed Association of American Painters and Sculptors at the Sixty-ninth Regiment Armory in New York City from February 17 to March 15. In perspective, Mr. Lloyd's assertion was less sweeping than it could have been. Not since 1913 has any art exhibit caused such hubbub and chatter.

The exhibit consisted of some 1,100 paintings, drawings, and sculptures by Americans and Europeans purporting to illustrate the "advance" from Ingres and Courbet through Cézanne, Manet, Gaugin, and Van Gogh to Matisse and the Post-Impressionists, and finally to the Cubist "incoherencies" of Picasso, Picabia, and Marcel Duchamp. The exhibit aroused so much anticipatory interest that the *Chicago Tribune* sent Harriet Monroe, founder and editor of *Poetry*, to New York to report it. On the whole, Miss Monroe approved. She admired the cosmopolitan character of the paintings and sculptures, the disregard of fusty academic standards, the enthusiasm, the exuberance that it represented. "Even the cubists," she wrote, "seem to be playing interesting games with kaleidoscopic polygons of color; even Matisse is dancing a wild tango on some weird barbarous shore. We cannot always tell what they mean, but at least they are having a good time."

The public reaction was something different. Miss Monroe reported the opinion of a visitor whom she characterized as a connoisseur:

"I can't laugh at that kind of insanity. . . . Something must be wrong with an age which can put those things in a gallery and call them art. The minds that produce them are fit subjects for alienists."

"What is it, Mother?" a ten-year-old asked. "Is it playing with blocks?"

"The grandest joke of the age," was the verdict of a well-groomed businessman.

Perhaps the most tolerant comment came from a woman attired in the slimmest of gowns and the thickest of furs:

"I'll buy some for my husband—this is art for the tired business man."

More than any other artist, Matisse aroused the ire of visitors. Miss Lucia Fairchild Fuller, a miniature painter, allowed herself to be quoted:

"I can't see why this person is tolerated. I believe the

critics don't dare speak the truth about his abominable monstrosities; they're afraid of being caught again as they were with Corot and Manet and Renoir years ago. He ought to be pilloried."

In her third and last article, Miss Monroe proved herself to be a prophet. The Association of American Painters and Sculptors, she wrote, deserved the highest commendation. Depending entirely on voluntary contributions, they had hired an armory—the only building in New York large enough for what they wanted to do—and with partitions and burlap had created an admirable setting. "With little fuss or funds they throw a bomb into the entrenched camps, give to American art a much needed shaking up, and achieve a live show which is sure of far-reaching influence."

In four weeks in New York 56,000 visitors saw the Armory Show and bought 200 paintings and sculptures ranging in price from $100 to $2,000.

On March 24 a curtailed Armory exhibit—453 paintings and sculptures from the original show—opened at the Art Institute of Chicago. Society turned out in force for a preview and confessed its collective mystification. No indecision marked the attitude of the city's art students. A few days after the exhibit opened the Chicago Artists' Club staged a "Futuristic Party" at the Art Institute. Pictures with such titles as "Chicago Artists Going to Hell," "Stewed Descending Staircase," and "Ace and Ten Spots Surrounded by Nudes" adorned the walls. Girls dressed their hair in excelsior and shavings, painted their faces in weird shades, and decked themselves in outlandish costumes. Mme. Pogany, a far-out sculpture by Brancusi, appeared with her face draped into the contour of an ostrich egg. "A man with a bale of shingles fastened to his clothes," the *Tribune* reported, "danced with a girl whose face represented a spider web, or a map of a railroad yard on a foggy night."

The orchestra played and the artists sang:

"I live in a madhouse over on the hills,
And play in the meadows with the daffydills,
I'm going crazy—don't you want to come along?"

When the Art Institute shipped the show to Boston the Chicago students held a solemn ceremony. Matisse, impersonated by one of their number, was tried on charges of "artistic murder, pictorial arson, artistic rapine, total degeneracy of color, criminal misuse of line, general esthetic aberration, and contumacious abuse of title," and found guilty. As punishment, copies of three of his paintings that had been left behind—"Luxury," "The Goldfish," and "The Blue Lady"—were burned.

Such antics might have been accounted for by the essential crudity of the hog butcher of the world, but the attitude they exemplified differed little from that of the Bostonians. "If the majority of the works in this exhibition were conceded to be works of art," the *Transcript* commented, "one would have no other alternative but to spurn art, and to do what might be possible to stamp it out as a pest."

The critic of the *Transcript* had words of faint praise for Cezanne, Van Gogh, and Gauguin—they were men of artistic integrity, though only "measurably successful" in attaining their purposes—but Matisse was nothing more than a mountebank, and there was no reason for taking him seriously. "We must surely agree with the art students of Chicago, who found him 'guilty of everything in the first degree,' and condemned him to death—a work of supererogation, since he has already committed artistic suicide."

A. J. Philpott, in the *Boston Globe,* was even more severe. One summary sentence in his review of the opening expressed his considered opinion: "There is scarcely a picture or a bit of sculpture in the exhibition that does not appear to be either an intentional joke, the work of an unbalanced mind, or the work of an extremely bad artist."

As the furor subsided, more balanced judgments began to appear in print. An editorial in *The Independent* suggested that much of the adverse reaction could be attributed to the titles given to the paintings. Had "Nude Descending a Staircase" been called "An Explosion in a Shingle Factory" there would have been little ground for ridicule. Considered simply as painted canvas and not as representations of anything, the paintings would have aroused little criticism—and attracted little attention.

David Lloyd, writing in the *American Year Book,* conceded that the Armory Show was in many respects a notable venture. The National Academy had become stodgy, and revolt against its standards was natural. After all, violent criticism focused on only a small fraction of the exhibit, and even the criticism served to interest many thousands in art for the first time in their lives.

Nevertheless, it is probable that a parody of "Danny Deever," by Edwin W. Goodwin, which *The Independent* printed in its issue for March 20, expressed better than hundreds of columns of critical prose the general attitude toward the new art.

"What are the Cubists painting for?" said Critics-on-Parade.
"Can't make it out, can't make it out," the Art Reporter said.
"What makes you look so white, so white?" said Critics-on-Parade.
"I'm dreading what I've got to watch," the Art Reporter said:

For they're hanging of the Cubists, you can see the the colors gay,
Green pyramids and yellow squares, they're hanging them today,
'Twould make you burst your buttons off, the things the people say.
And they're hanging of the Cubists in the morning.

"What makes the rear rank breathe so hard," said Critics-on-Parade.
"He thinks they're sold! He thinks they're sold," the Art Reporter said.

They are hanging of the Cubists, and the crowds are marching round,
They've halted by what seems to be a Brainstorm done in brown;
And they'll swear in half a minute that they've hung it upside down.
Oh, they're hanging of the Cubists in the morning!

"What's that so black against the sun?" said Critics-on-Parade.

"They *say* it is a flight of stairs," the Art Reporter said.
"What's all that wreckage overhead?" said Critics-on-Parade.
"A 'cubic' nude is passing down," the Art Reporter said.

For they've finished with the Cubists, you can feel your hair's turned gray,
The visitors are in column, and they're marching them away,
Ho! The nervous ones are shaking, and they'll want their beer today,
After viewing of the Cubists in the morning![1]

The record does not show any effort by the police to "suppress" any of the paintings in the Armory Show. But when the proprietor of a Chicago art shop exhibited a life-size color reproduction of Paul Chabas' "September Morn" the law stepped in, ordered the painting removed, and arrested the exhibitor on a morals charge. When the case came up for trial Mrs. Ella Flagg Young, Superintendent

[1] *The* Chicago Daily News, *January 23, 1963: "The liveliest dialog in town is heard within the Morton Wing of the Art Institute where contemporary paintings and sculpture have attracted hundreds of artists, students and amateur critics during the first week of the 66th Annual American Exhibition. . . . The dash of the new idiom seemed most felt at the sight of the top prize winner in sculpture, for no one failed to pause to look at 'Tom,' a large assembly made of old timbers and boards, metal pipe and ropes, stretching 10 feet either way and 8 feet high. This work by Mark di Suvero won a Logan Medal with $1,000. . . .*

"Passersby gave audible judgments on the whole show: 'It's metaphysical,' said an earnest man. A woman said: 'This is the end of painting.' One man, looking at one object, said: 'Maybe I'm crazy.'"

of Schools, obviously uncomfortable, testified that she did not think that children under fourteen should be permitted to view even a picture of a nude young woman. Miss Harriet Monroe, also put on the stand, considered "September Morn" harmless. The jury—all men, of course—agreed with Miss Monroe and found the dealer not guilty. He promptly presented each juror with one of the reproductions that had caused the fuss.

Early on the morning of Sunday, March 2, crowds began pouring into Washington. Every track entering the Union Station was solid with special trains discharging hordes of politicians, suffragettes, soldiers, and tourists; other trains waited in the yards for space in the terminal. Carriages, automobiles, and "rubberneck wagons" stood in block-long lines around the station, each certain of a capacity load. Every available streetcar had been pressed into service, yet thousands had to make their way to hotels and boarding houses on foot. Although the inauguration was two days off, it was estimated that 50,000 people from other parts of the country had already found their way to the capital.

Conspicuous in the crowds were the Southerners, called the "big hat boys" because of their preference for wide-brimmed, black slouch hats. The military staffs of several governors, in fancy uniforms, attracted attention. National guardsmen, wearing discipline lightly, had bedecked their campaign hats with ribbons inscribed, "I Should Worry," or "Votes for Women."

Pennsylvania Avenue, from the Capitol grounds to the White House, had taken on a festival aspect. Festoons of red, white, and blue lights hung across the street at close intervals. The buildings were adorned with flags and bunting, and at night alive with elaborate designs of electric lights. In the distance the Washington Monument, with only its top illuminated, looked as if it were suspended from the sky.

A carnival mood prevailed. Bands and military companies marched and countermarched. Hawkers sold flags and banners, canes, whistles, and balloons. Merrymakers tooted horns. The Indiana Democratic Club marched to the Shoreham Hotel and serenaded Vice-President-elect Marshall with "On the Banks of the Wabash." And between 11:00 A.M. and 6:00 P.M., 125 drunks were carted to the Emergency Hospital.

Monday saw more visitors—and an unprecedented spectacle. The suffragettes of the country, sensing that the election of Wilson signified a national receptiveness to change, had decided to impress the incoming administration with a huge demonstration. From all over the country, even from abroad, thousands of members of the scores of organizations pressing for votes for women converged on Washington.

The parade was scheduled to start at 3:00 P.M. from the Peace Monument at the foot of Capitol Hill and proceed to the White House. Washington authorities, who had reluctantly granted a permit for the procession, failed to take anything like adequate measures to keep order, protect the women, and clear the line of march. Two hundred thousand people choked the route the procession was to follow. Miraculously, the marchers organized and the front rank stepped out only twenty minutes late. The marchers soon found themselves facing an almost impenetrable wall of humanity. Mounted police, far too few in number, tried to clear at least the center of the street; men in automobiles used bulldozer tactics. The crowd yelled and cursed, and flowed back into the cleared space as soon as the cars had passed.

During the afternoon seventy-five women, spectators as well as marchers, were taken to the Emergency Hospital, the victims of fainting spells, hysteria, or the iron-shod hooves of policemen's horses. One young woman lost her skirt in the crush, leading to what a reporter described as a considerable display of hosiery. A gallant young man lent an overcoat, and the woman was hurried to a nearby hotel, in hysterics.

Somehow, the suffragettes fought through the crowd—literally fought; one woman spurred her horse into the crowd as if she were leading a cavalry charge; another slashed a rowdy's face with a riding crop. At the head of the procession the girls' band of the Missouri Northwest Normal School blared out marches. Behind the girls rode young Mrs. Richard Burleson, wife of an army officer, on a crack cavalry mount. With her were two mounted "heralds": Miss Inez Mulholland and Miss Alberta Hill of New York; Miss Mulholland "one grand ecstasy in white, with a golden crown on her tresses"; Miss Hill wearing "natty tailored riding clothes and puttees and riding headgear designed along the lines of the colonial cocked hat." Behind the heralds came a troupe of young women, all in identical black riding habits.

A wide flat float bearing a huge placard: "We demand an amendment to the United States Constitution enfranchising the women of the country," followed the "cavalry."

Near the head of the procession a score of men braved the jeers of the crowd. At their head marched Congressman A. W. Rucker of Colorado carrying a banner with the legend, "Senators and Representatives from Suffrage States."

Dr. Anna Howard Shaw, president of the National Woman Suffrage Association, marched by herself. Following her, in one rank, came members of the national board: Mrs. Mary Ware Dennett and Mrs. Harriet Lees Laidlaw of New York, Mrs. Susan Fitzgerald of Boston, Mrs. Stanley McCormick of Boston and Chicago.

One section of floats represented the progress of the suffrage movement throughout the world. Women of Norway, Finland, New Zealand, and Australia represented the countries with equal suffrage. Floats of Sweden, Denmark, Iceland, Great Britain, and Belgium designated the countries in which women enjoyed a limited franchise. Several marchers impersonated the pioneers of the suffrage movement. Washingtonians agreed that the parade would have been one of the most impressive spectacles in the history of the capital had it not been for the incredible unpreparedness of the police and the covert hostility of higher authorities.

At the mass meeting in Continental Hall, where the parade disbanded, Dr. Shaw drew a moral from the experience of the afternoon. "I have marched in the streets of London, of Philadelphia, and in New York," she said,

Ford Motor Company

Ford Model T Runabout

Ford Motor Company

John Burroughs, the naturalist, in a Ford touring car, the gift of Henry Ford

You can make no better selection than to buy a Motor Truck of proven superiority in your own line of work.

Velie Trucks are made in three sizes to meet every possible requirement in Motor Truck service.

The Velie One - Ton Delivery Truck, equipped with electric lighting and starting, shows an economy in short hauls of relatively light loads not found in any other type of Motor Truck service.

The Velie Two-Ton Truck is especially adapted for expressage and general service.

For heavy hauls, where maximum loads are handled constantly, the Velie Three-Ton Truck finds this particular field.

Each in its own field of operation has established a record for economy and for general service, that is not equalled by that of any other type of Motor Truck.

A comparative study of Velie Motor Truck specifications with those of any other Motor Truck built will show you why.

Investigation among the list of Velie Truck owners, representing practically every kind of truck service in every part of the country, will be a final argument.

Send for special Truck folder concerning the model in which you are interested.

VELIE MOTOR VEHICLE COMPANY
52 Velie Place, MOLINE, ILL.

(28)

Literary Digest

Truck by a once-prosperous maker, long since disappeared

ary 8, 1913 THE LITERARY DIGEST

OVER fifteen thousand Overlands have been delivered during the last *five months.* This is *more* cars than *all* the automobile factories in Germany turn out in *a whole year.* This is an *increase* of 300 per cent. over the same period last year. And last year we *led* every thousand dollar automobile producer in America. Our 1913 sales are more than *double* those of any other manufacturer producing a similar car.

In such states as Minnesota, one of the *largest* automobile consuming States in the Union, the Overland has shown a *larger increase* this year than *any* other motor car manufactured *—bar none.*

The Overland *outsells* because it *outclasses.* Overland value is *better* because it is *bigger.* You get *more* car for *less* money.

Catalogue on request. Please address Dept. 17

The Willys-Overland Company, Toledo, Ohio

$985—Completely Equipped

Model 69-T

Self-starter
30 Horse Power
5-Passenger Touring Car
110-inch Wheel Base

Timken Bearings
Center Control
Remy Magneto
Warner Speedometer

Mohair Top and Boot
Clear Vision, Rain Vision
Wind Shield
Prest-O-Lite Tank

Literary Digest

A popular higher-priced car

Sears Roebuck Catalog

Still a good seller at Sears Roebuck

Daily News Photo, Chicago Historical Society

Auto racers: Eddie Rickenbacker, left, and Eddie O'Donell

Culver Pictures, Inc.

Glenn Curtiss and his flying boat with Henry Ford at Hammondsport, N.Y., Curtiss' home

Daily News Photo, Chicago Historical Society

Glenn Martin coming down at Chicago

Chicago Tribune

John T. McCutcheon tells the story of aviation in the United States

Daily News Photo, Chicago Historical Society

Jim Thorpe, trophies gone, puts on a Giant uniform

Culver Pictures, Inc.

Billy Sunday hammering home the message

Brown Brothers

Billy Sunday before a typical revival meeting

Philadelphia Museum of Art

Marcel Duchamp, "Nude Descending a Staircase." The "hit" of the Armory Show?

The Museum of Modern Art

Henri Matisse, "The Red Studio." They found him guilty of everything

The Metropolitan Museum of Art

Paul Chabas, "September Morn." Fit for children to see? Or even adults?

Culver Pictures, Inc.

Four suffragettes on the march to Washington

Culver Pictures, Inc.

Suffragettes gathering in New York for the march to Washington

Brown Brothers

Miss Inez Mulholland, "one grand ecstasy in white," heads the Washington suffrage parade

Brown Brothers

The suffrage marchers make a brave start

Culver Pictures, Inc

Wilson and Taft at the White House, ready to leave for the inauguration

Daily News Photo, Chicago Historical Society

West Point Cadets arriving at the scene of the inauguration.
Foreground: Culver Military Academy's Black Horse Troop

Daily News Photo, Chicago Historical Society

Wilson takes the oath of office

Daily News Photo, Chicago Historical Society

Wilson and Taft after the inauguration. Who was happier?

THE MINIMUM WAGE

"MY DEAR YOUNG LADY, I HOPE YOU PRAY GOD EVERY NIGHT TO KEEP YOU A GOOD GIRL."
"I DON'T HAVE TO. I GET EIGHT DOLLARS A WEEK."

Life

Could eight dollars a week keep a woman virtuous?

Brown Brothers

J. P. Morgan, with Mrs. Morgan, near the end of his life

Daily News Photo, Chicago Historical Societ

Wreckage left by the Omaha tornado

Daily News Photo, Chicago Historical Society

An Omaha street, after the tornado

Daily News Photo, Chicago Historical Society

Peru, Indiana, under water

Dayton Daily News

Downtown Dayton under water

Dayton Daily News

Dayton, Ohio, after the flood receded

Drawn by C. R. Weed.

THE MAN WHO PUT THE "DENT" IN *PRECEDENT*

929

The Independent

Wilson about to break a precedent, April 8

Chicago Historical Society

John T. McCutcheon, Chicago Tribune, on the old and new styles in presidential messages "and never in my life have I seen such an exhibition of incompetency as I have seen today in the streets of the nation's capital." The experience of the afternoon should prove to any doubter, she declared, that women needed the ballot to insure for themselves the protection that would be accorded men on the following day.

Miss Helen Keller, blind, deaf, and famous at thirty-three for her success in overcoming these handicaps, could not address the meeting because of the rough treatment she had received from the crowds in the afternoon.

While the suffragettes pushed their way along Pennsylvania Avenue, Woodrow Wilson and his family, riding a special train made up principally of Princeton students, arrived at the Union Station. Only a few of the faithful were on hand to welcome him: as an attraction the suffrage parade outweighed the advent of a new President. Carried immediately to the Shoreham Hotel, the President-elect and his wife were greeted by Mr. and Mrs. Marshall, the men designated as members of the Cabinet, and Democratic leaders of the House and Senate. The reception over, the Wilsons drove to the White House for a courtesy call on President and Mrs. Taft. A half hour later the Tafts, observing the amenities punctiliously, appeared at the Shoreham for a brief call on their successors. That evening Wilson attended a banquet of 800 Princeton alumni at the Willard Hotel. When he arose, and after the applause had subsided, his voice was unsteady with feeling. He hadn't intended to say anything, he admitted, because there were emotions deeper than words could reach. But he could not hold to his resolution.

"We have often spoken of our comradeship together as Princeton men, and I have spoken so often that I am ashamed almost to repeat it, of the part that Princeton has played in public life and the part that she ought to play in public life. As I stand here upon the eve of attempting a great task, I rejoice that there are so many men in the United States who know me and understand me and to whom I do not have to explain everything. . . .

"I thank God that it is so, and thank you profoundly for this evidence of it."

On the morning of March 4 a wan sun shone through the haze enveloping the capital. As the hours passed the air cleared and the temperature rose until at noon the thermometer stood at 60° in the shade. Given the time of year, no one could have expected finer weather.

The Senate, which had sat until four o'clock in the morning, had been called to meet at 9:30 A.M., but it was 11:30 before the members were in their seats and ready for the business of the day. As the crowded galleries fidgeted in expectation, a young man in a frock coat moved down the center aisle and announced to the presiding officer, Senator Gallinger of New Hampshire: "The President directs me to present to Congress a message in writing." The reading of the message—a veto of an appropriations bill—took several minutes. At the conclusion Senator Poindexter of Washington gained the floor and launched into an attack on the Washington police for their failure to protect the suffragettes in the parade on the preceding day. Senators looked at the clock with apprehension; the clerk scurried around the chamber and turned back the hands a half an hour. Finally the Senator sat down. The members of the House of Representatives entered the chamber, the diplomatic corps in bemedalled, colorful uniforms filed in, then the justices of the Supreme Court in their somber gowns.

As soon as the justices were seated the sergeant-at-arms announced: "The Vice-President-elect of the United States." A minute later came the announcement for which all had been waiting: "The President of the United States and the President-elect."

Wearing a black frock coat and striped trousers, features solemn, eyes straight ahead, Woodrow Wilson walked to the front of the chamber beside the rotund Taft, who, aware of the trials and frustrations that awaited his successor, permitted himself the ghost of a smile.

Without delay Senator Gallinger administered the oath to Marshall, made a brief farewell speech of his own, turned the gavel over to the new Vice-President, and announced that the Sixty-second Congress was adjourned *sine die*.

The occupants of the Senate chamber moved to the east portico of the Capitol, where a stand large enough to accommodate 10,000 people had been erected. Facing the platform stood a seemingly endless crowd extending, in the center, as far as the Library of Congress, and on the sides to the House and Senate office buildings. Every tree, every statue, held aloft a capacity load of boys and men; the roof of the Capitol and the balconies on the dome were jammed with humanity. No previous inauguration had attracted so many spectators.

As Taft and Wilson came out from the Capitol and mounted the small raised platform on which the oath was to be administered the audience cheered, though without verve. The real demonstration greeted William Jennings Bryan as he moved to take his seat. Embarrassed, the Commoner turned his back to the crowd in an effort to discourage an ovation greater than that which had greeted his chief.

In front of the platform a considerable space had been kept clear, with the crowd held back by West Point cadets and midshipmen from Annapolis. From the rostrum Wilson motioned to a guard. "Let the people come forward," he ordered. The cadets and the midshipmen wheeled, moved off in perfect order, and the people came forward with a rush. In months to come "Let the people come forward" would be the slogan of ardent proponents of the New Freedom.

It was just 1:30 when President Taft signaled to the crowd for silence. Chief Justice White, venerable Confederate veteran, clad in black gown and skull cap, motioned to Wilson. While both men held their hands on an open Bible, the jurist recited the oath:

"I do solemnly swear that I will faithfully execute the office of President of the United States and will to the best of my ability preserve, protect, and defend the Constitution of the United States."

"I do," Wilson responded with fervor, and then bent to kiss the open book.

The new President faced the crowd, his manuscript in his right hand.

"My fellow citizens," he began in a strong, clear voice, "there has been a change of government. . . . What does the change mean? That is the question that is uppermost in our minds today. That is the question I am going to try to answer. . . ."

The success of the Democratic Party, in his interpretation, meant that the people of the country had taken a fresh and critical look at institutions and practices which they had long accepted with little question. In many aspects of national life they found true greatness. They found great wealth, energy, and moral force. They found willingness to rectify wrong, to alleviate suffering, to help the weak and unfortunate. And they found a system of government that was a model for those everywhere who would set liberty upon a firm foundation.

"Our life contains every great thing, and contains it in rich abundance," the President asserted.

"But the evil has come with the good," he continued, "and much fine gold has been corroded." We have squandered a great part of our natural resources. We have not counted the human cost of our industrial achievements. The government has been used too often for private and selfish purposes. "We remembered well enough that we had set up a policy which was meant to serve the humblest as well as the most powerful, with an eye single to the standards of justice and fair play, and remembered it with pride. But we were very heedless and in a hurry to be great."

The time had come for change and restoration; specifically, tariff reform, a banking and currency system adapted to present-day needs, an industrial system which would exploit neither labor nor the public, the conservation of national resources. Above all, the government must be put at the service of humanity.

"This is the high enterprise of the new day: to lift everything that concerns our life as a Nation to the light that shines from the hearthfires of every man's conscience and vision of the right. . . . It is inconceivable we should do it in ignorance of the facts as they are or in blind haste. We shall restore, not destroy. . . . Justice, and only justice, shall always be our motto."

The President had spoken for no more than fifteen minutes, yet he had come to his conclusion:

"This is not a day of triumph; it is a day of dedication. Here muster, not the forces of party, but the forces of humanity. Men's hearts wait upon us; men's lives hang in the balance; men's hopes call upon us to say what we will do. Who shall live up to the great trust? Who dares fail to try? I summon all honest men, all patriotic, all forward-looking men, to my side. God helping me, I will not fail them, if they will but counsel and sustain me!"

The thunder of applause came from the great crowd, although only a few thousand could have heard the President's words.

Wilson and Taft returned to the White House. After a quick luncheon the President took his place on the reviewing stand. For four hours he watched the longest inaugural parade in history: units of every branch of the armed services, national guardsmen, governors and their staffs, independent militia companies in gaudy uniforms, political marching clubs, a delegation of Indian chiefs on ponies, and near the end, a thousand howling, cheering Princetonians. It was 7:00 P.M. before the President could walk across the dark lawn to his new home.

That night Washington was dressed in lights as never before. A salute of 101 guns drew thousands to the vicinity of the Washington Monument, where for two hours they witnessed an extravagant display of fireworks. At 11:30 a series of bombs exploded high in the air and formed in immense letters the names, "Wilson" and "Marshall." More bombs, and the words "Good Night." By midnight the streets began to lapse into darkness. The white dome of the Capitol and the shaft of the Washington Monument disappeared. The Peace Monument ceased its splashing, and Pennsylvania Avenue became again its dingy, dimly-lighted self.

The Literary Digest, polling the press of the country, concluded that not since the days of Lincoln had the nation heard a finer expression of American idealism. Wilson, some editors said, possessed the ability to stir the hearts of men as well as their minds.

Expressions of approval ranged from the comment of the *New York Times:* "No President of the United States in any utterance ever sounded a higher or clearer note of aspiration and of idealism," to the earthy remark of the Louisville *Courier-Journal:* "Assuredly the new President has the right pig by the ear." Some foresaw the early break-up of the Progressive Party—the scholar from Princeton had stolen its thunder. The only reproach came from a handful of editors who had hoped for a more specific legislative program than that which the President announced.

Even before the inauguration knowledgable newspapermen had revealed the composition of Wilson's Cabinet. On March 4 their divinations were confirmed.

Secretary of State: William Jennings Bryan of Nebraska, lawyer, editor, leader of the Democratic Party from 1896 to 1912, and three times its unsuccessful candidate for the Presidency.

Secretary of the Treasury: William G. McAdoo of New York, lawyer and industrialist.

Attorney General: James C. McReynolds of New York, formerly of Tennessee, lawyer.

Secretary of War: Lindley Miller Garrison of New Jersey, lawyer, and vice-chancellor of his state.

Secretary of the Navy: Josephus Daniels of North Carolina, newspaper editor.

Secretary of the Interior: Franklin K. Lane of California, former newspaperman; since 1905 member of the Interstate Commerce Commission.

Secretary of Commerce: William C. Redfield of New York, manufacturer, member of the 62nd Congress (1911–13).

Secretary of Agriculture: David F. Houston of Missouri, educator, chancellor of Washington University, St. Louis.

Secretary of Labor (a department created in the last days of the Taft administration): William B. Wilson of Pennsylvania, labor leader.

Postmaster General: Albert S. Burleson of Texas, lawyer and veteran Congressman.

The Cabinet was not the one which Wilson would have

chosen had he had a free hand. But a President never has a free hand in the selection of his cabinet; political debts must be paid, geographical requirements met. Wilson had little faith in Bryan's judgment, and he knew that his appointment would alarm the business and financial leaders of the country. He also knew that Bryan remained the idol of millions of Democrats, and that the party would be badly ruptured if he were not given the highest post at the command of the administration. Wilson finally reconciled himself to the inevitable.

In the appointment of McAdoo, Wilson defied political considerations. William F. McCombs, chairman of the Democratic National Committee, wanted the Treasury, and by the rules of the game deserved a cabinet post. But Wilson disliked and distrusted McCombs, and refused, despite pressures, to offer him more than an embassy. The situation was complicated by the fact that McCombs hated McAdoo. McCombs, his ambition thwarted, refused the foreign post, retained the party chairmanship, and went into a prolonged and petulant sulk.

For Attorney General, Wilson had set his heart on Louis D. Brandeis. This Boston lawyer had made a reputation as a sharp critic of monopoly and economic privilege. During the campaign he had been Wilson's most trusted adviser. But the President-elect soon found out that no prominent man had more enemies than Brandeis. Big business would accept Bryan, though reluctantly; at rumors of the Brandeis appointment protests flooded Trenton. There were even reports of personal dishonesty to which, strange as it may seem today, Wilson gave some credence. Finally the President yielded and allowed his intimate counselor, Edward M. House, to name James

McReynolds, whom he had never met, to the post.

Balked in his desire to make Brandeis Attorney General, Wilson considered him for Secretary of Commerce. That the President-elect could convince himself that the business leaders of the country would acquiesce in a man at the head of the Department of Commerce whom they would not accept as Attorney General was a sign of his own naiveté. They soon disillusioned him. Redfield, a Brooklyn manufacturer who was known to favor lower tariffs, was selected. Having a limited reputation, no one knew enough about him—or cared enough—to offer any opposition.

The appointment of Josephus Daniels to the Navy Department was an unabashed political reward. Editor of the Raleigh (North Carolina) *News and Observer,* he had served as director of publicity in the 1912 campaign. The fact that nothing in his experience qualified him for the position was not considered. (In fact, he would turn out to be a very able department head.)

The choice of Garrison for the War Department came about by pure chance. After having decided upon Franklin K. Lane for the Interior, Wilson decided to shift him to the War Department, and give the Interior to Walter Hines Page, editor of the *World's Work* and a member of the publishing firm of Doubleday, Page & Company. The plan was abandoned when it was pointed out that Page had come from North Carolina, and that no Southerner could be put in charge of a department—the Interior—that dispensed pensions to Union veterans. Wilson turned to A. Mitchell Palmer, a well known Pennsylvania lawyer, for War. Palmer declined. He was a member of the Society of Friends, he informed Wilson, and "as a Quaker

War Secretary I should consider myself a living illustration of a horrible incongruity." As late as March 1 no choice had been made. On that day Joseph P. Tumulty, whom Wilson had already named as his secretary, was idly leafing through a New Jersey lawyer's directory. His eye fell on Garrison's name, and he immediately suggested him to Wilson. Garrison protested that nothing in his experience qualified him for the position, but Wilson overrode his objection.

For the Interior, Wilson had wanted Newton D. Baker of Ohio. But Baker, recently elected Mayor of Cleveland, took the position that he had made a contract with the voters which he could not abrogate. The President-elect then took Franklin K. Lane on House's recommendation. The two men—Wilson and Lane—did not meet until inauguration day.

Houston, for Secretary of Agriculture, was the choice of House. For Secretary of Labor William B. Wilson seemed obvious. He was a former secretary of the United Mine Workers, he had been a Democratic Representative from Pennsylvania, and he had introduced the bill creating the department.

Albert S. Burleson could attribute his appointment as Postmaster General, traditionally the patronage dispenser of an administration, partly to the influence of geography, and partly to the favor of his fellow members of the House of Representatives, in which he had served since 1899. He came from Texas, where the progressive Democratic vote had been heavy. His colleagues, who knew him as a shrewd politician, wanted someone in the Cabinet who could present what they considered their just political claims to a scholar-President who, they feared, would not be inclined to pass out rewards. In spite of Wilson's reluctance to draw on Congress for cabinet material, they had their way.

In *The New Freedom,* which contains the essence of Wilson's objectives and plans as he propounded them during the campaign of 1912, there is not a single direct reference to foreign relations. But one brief passage holds the clue to the policy which he would be called upon to formulate without delay. "What," he asked, "was in the writings of the men who founded America—to serve the selfish interests of America? Do you find that in their writings? No; to serve the cause of humanity, to bring liberty to mankind."

In his first week in office Wilson was faced with foreign problems which pressed for attention: the revolution in Mexico, Colombia's demand for satisfaction over the "theft" of Panama, negotiations with Nicaragua for a canal route through that country, an impasse with Great Britain over the right of foreign nations to use the Panama Canal on the same terms as the United States. There could be no delay, he decided, in clarifying the position of the administration.

On March 10 the President typed out a statement. He had consulted no one, not even his Secretary of State. The following day he read it to the Cabinet. "One of the chief objects of my administration," he began, "will be to cultivate the friendship and deserve the confidence of our sister republics of Central and South America, and to promote in every proper and honorable way the interests which are common to the people of the two continents." To this end he hoped for understanding and co-operation between the nations of the continent. Co-operation, however, was possible only when supported by governments "based upon law, not upon arbitrary or irregular force," governments resting always upon the consent of the governed.

That statement concluded:

"The United States has nothing to seek in Central and South America except the lasting interests of the peoples of the two continents, the security of governments intended for the people and for no special group or interest, and the development of personal and trade relationships between the two continents which shall redound to the profit and advantage of both and interfere with the rights and liberties of neither."

Several members of the Cabinet demurred: The statement was hasty; it had been prepared without consultation; it might be considered the work of amateurs. The President, after listening patiently to the objections, answered that agitators in certain countries wanted to foment revolutions and believed that they could get away with them before the new administration was firmly established. As far as he was concerned, they wouldn't. With that comment, he gave the statement to the press, to be published the next day, March 12.

Experienced diplomats may have smiled at the Professor's naiveté, but the reaction in the United States was almost wholly favorable. The statement was audacious, impressive, and could give no offense; it was evidence that the administration would neither be hoodwinked nor trifled with; it should dash the hopes of the exploiters, the "marauding corporations," and the dictators disguised as deliverers. George Harvey, writing at the time in *Harper's Weekly,* appraised the statement in a sentence: "No act of any President in twenty years has produced results more immediately beneficial, from combined reassurance and indicated resoluteness, than this initial act of President Wilson." Nearly twenty years later Ray Stannard Baker could write: "It was amateur diplomacy with a vengeance: but there was somehow mastery in it."

Wilson's statement of policy on the United States and Latin America was readily applicable to a pressing Far Eastern problem. Two years earlier bankers in the United States, Great Britain, France, and Germany had joined forces to make what were to them extremely favorable railroad and currency loans to China's tottering government. Arrangements, completed in 1911, were a factor in touching off the Chinese revolution of that year, but the eager lenders were not dismayed. In fact, they enlarged their group by admitting Russia and Japan. American participation, principally J. P. Morgan and Company and Kuhn, Loeb and Company, had the blessing of the Taft administration.

But the new administration was an unknown quantity. In its first week two Morgan partners called on Bryan. Would the State Department follow the policy of the previous administration and approve the China loan? Bryan, who had never heard of the Six Power Consortium, called

Assistant Secretary Huntington Wilson and Counsellor Chandler P. Anderson, both Taft appointees, into the conference. Both argued strongly in favor of government support. Bryan was noncommittal, but brought up the subject at the next Cabinet meeting. At that time he admitted that he had no very clear notion of the situation but he promised to be fully informed by March 18, when another meeting was to be held.

At that time the Secretary of State reported that the terms of the loan included participation by foreign officers in the Chinese financial administration and sanctioned the use of force if necessary for the collection of interest and payments on principal. This was clearly an invasion of the independence of another nation, and Bryan, as staunch a moralist as his chief, advised against American involvement. He found Wilson in full accord. In fact, the President had come to the Cabinet meeting with a prepared statement. He too foresaw that the conditions of the loan might require American interference—even forcible interference—in the affairs of another state, and this would be particularly repugnant when that state was just "awakening to a consciousness of its power and of its obligations to its people." Such responsibilities as the loan implied were obnoxious to American principles.

The Cabinet agreed. Huntington Wilson resigned in anger. The American bankers immediately withdrew from the Consortium. And on May 2, the United States recognized the Republic of China.

Theodore Roosevelt to a fifth cousin:

"Oyster Bay, March 18, 1913

"Dear Franklin: I was very much pleased to see that you were appointed as Assistant Secretary of the Navy. It is interesting to see that you are in another place which I myself once held. I am sure you will enjoy yourself to the full as Assistant Secretary of the Navy, and that you will do capital work. When I see Eleanor I shall say to her that I do hope she will be particularly nice to the naval officers' wives. They have a pretty hard time, with very little money to get along on, and yet a position to keep up, and everything that can properly be done to make things pleasant for them should be done. . . ."

Fifty years ago a great many Americans were obsessed with the subject of irregular sexual relations, and had no trouble in finding contributing causes in everything from the peek-a-boo waist to "Alexander's Ragtime Band." When the Illinois State Senate appointed a commission to investigate the question of a minimum wage for women, the inquiry inevitably took up the relationship between low wages and vice, or "white slavery" in the terminology of the day.

(The investigation was given added zest early in the proceedings when the chairman of the commission was accused of having picked up a woman of the evening on the train from Springfield to Chicago and with having spent the night in her room. A Springfield citizen who enjoyed, in both senses of the word, a reputation for unconventional behavior, came to the chairman's rescue. He had been with him all evening. Together, they had met the lady in question, and had had two or three drinks after arriving in Chicago. The chairman then departed and had no share in what happened afterward.)[1]

Early in March the great merchants of Chicago testified as to the wages paid to women and girls in their establishments. Julius Rosenwald, president of Sears, Roebuck and Company, stated that his firm employed about 4,700 women, whose weekly wages averaged $9.12. Edward F. Mandel, of Mandel Brothers, employing 1,866 women, gave their average weekly wage as $9.86. Other executives —James Simpson, vice-president of Marshall Field and Company, Joseph Basch, vice-president of Siegel Cooper and Company, Henry C. Lytton of The Hub—corroborated the testimony of Messrs. Rosenwald and Mandel. But these figures were averages. All admitted that they employed many girls for as little as $5.00 a week. And these were the wages paid in the large and prosperous businesses. The scale in the smaller establishment was lower.

In the course of a short-lived garment workers' strike in New York earlier in the year Theodore Roosevelt had made his own investigation of the wages paid to young women. On January 24 he had reported his findings to Michael A. Schaap, Progressive floor leader in the New York Assembly. With Roosevelt's consent, Schaap gave the letter to the New York newspapers:

"I visited bodies of girl strikers in Henry Street and in St. Mark's Place, and choosing at random listened to the stories of the different girls. In Henry Street the girls were

[1] *The author, who knew the gallant Springfielder, believes that he told the truth.*

mostly recent immigrants from Southern Spain and from the Turkish Empire. Those from the Turkish Empire could not speak English, and although they were of the Jewish faith they could not speak Yiddish, so that they were peculiarly helpless under our conditions here. Some of the girls were fourteen and fifteen years old, others sixteen, seventeen and eighteen. The wages were in one or two cases as low as $3 a week, and up to $5.50, $6, and $8 a week. I was informed that there were girls who worked for $2.50 a week, and there was one I saw who worked for $3.31 a week, and two or three who worked for $3 a week. One girl of fifteen earned $5 a week, but had to pay $30 for a machine on which she worked. Another, who had to pay $32 for a machine, worked from 8 A.M. to 8 P.M. and mentioned that in Summer she was charged 10 cents a week for ice water. Another girl who was earning $5 a week had a father in the hospital, and out of the $5 a week was supporting two young children, her brother and sister, in addition to herself. . . .

"In St. Mark's Place the girls looked healthier and as if their lives were lived under better conditions—better conditions of course being a purely relative term, for the conditions as to many of the girls were very bad also. They spoke English. Many of these girls did not live at their homes, and in such cases the owner of the house in which they lived, whom they generally spoke of as the 'missus,' charged them $3 a month for lodging, this lodging sometimes consisting of one bed and sometimes of a place in a bed with other girls. I was informed that often three or four girls slept in one bed. One such girl, for instance, was earning $4.50 a week, $18 a month. Out of this she paid $3 for lodging, $2 a week or $9.50 a month for breakfast and supper; leaving $6 a month for dinner or the mid-day meal, for carfare, for clothing, for medicine when sick, for dentist, for oculist, as well as for recreation if there was any. I mention the oculist particularly because the conditions of work are such that the eyes of many of the girls are affected."

The Chicago merchants agreed that a girl could not support herself on less than $8.00 a week, and to live on that sum she had to practice the most rigorous economy. William C. Thorne, vice-president of Montgomery Ward and Company, itemized the expenses of a woman living by herself as follows:

Room rent	$3.00
Breakfasts	.40
Luncheons	.90
Dinners	1.40
Carfare	.60
Clothing and incidentals	1.70
	$8.00

Mr. Simpson backed up Mr. Thorne, but experienced social workers contended that $12.00 represented the minimum.

All the employers were convinced that there was no connection between the wages they paid and commercialized vice. Girls would be good girls or bad girls according to their inclinations, and financial considerations were unimportant. Mr. Simpson, of Marshall Field and Company, told the commission that "an infinitesimal percentage of women go wrong the first time for monetary reasons." Julius Rosenwald saw "practically no connection between low wages and prostitution." Mr. Basch, of Siegel

Cooper and Company, saw immorality as "a state of mind" rather than the result of financial compulsions.

All were agreed, too, that an increase in the minimum wage rate for women would drive more of them into white slavery. According to Henry Siegel, of Siegel Cooper and Company's New York office, a legal minimum wage of no more than $9.00 a week would drive many women out of work. "Then it may be said truly," Mr. Siegel testified, "that industry has forced them to the streets. A man at $12.00 is more valuable than a woman at $7.00 or $9.00. . . . Men would take their places at slight increases."

The chairman of the commission disagreed. In his opinion, the hearings proved that low wages were to blame for most of the immorality among young girls, and the only cure was a law prescribing a minimum rate of pay. With this conclusion *The Nation* took issue. "It implies not only a general want of character which is a gross libel on the vast majority of women, but is contrary to the obvious facts of life. To choose a life of shame in preference to living on six dollars a week means not only want of virtue, but want of sense. . . . And life upon $8 a week, or $12 a week, is not so delightful as to remove the influence of these temptations and weaknesses."

With this point of view the General Assembly of Illinois, and the legislatures of a dozen other states which had appointed similar commissions, agreed.

The connection between low wages for women and sin had to be guessed at, but anyone could see that the increasing "immodesty" of women's clothes was bound to excite the base nature of the male half of American humanity. The *Ladies Home Journal* made the point explicitly in its April issue:

"We must not forget that there is a distinct point of morals in this question of how a girl dresses. When we see young girls . . . brazenly or innocently displaying in their attire their physical rather than their innocent charms, the fault is not so much with the girls as it is with the mothers. . . . When a girl is permitted to buy and wear the amazing hats that she wore last year, set on a head loaded down with puffs and 'rats,' the waist so thin and transparent as to be absolutely indecent, with sleeves so short and neck so low as to transgress the line of decency, and a skirt so tight that the figure is displayed at every step, with stockings of the thinnest transparent silk, there is a question of morals involved that is tremendous."

The slit skirt came in for the most vigorous condemnation. Everywhere women, mothers as well as daughters, were revealing a length of silk-clad leg varying from ankle to mid-calf or, among the bolder, to the knee. Some attributed the fashion to the motor car, which a hobbled woman could enter or leave only with the greatest difficulty; some to the new dances; some to the evil machinations of Paris designers. (The French, everyone knew, were congenitally licentious.)

One suspects that much of the disapproval of the slit skirt came not from the revelation it offered, but from the well-founded assumption that under a slit skirt slips and petticoats had to be reduced to a minimum, if worn at all. One of the causes of the Paterson silk workers' strike was diminished demand for silk caused by the curtailment of women's gowns. It is hard to see, from the fashion pictures of the day, how the gowns themselves had been curtailed. Something else must have been eliminated. Occasional news stories support the hypothesis. A typical one came from Lima, Ohio, where a woman whose skirt was slit from ankle to the knee, with "a stream of afternoon sunlight filtering through her tight, clinging raiment, silhouetting her form," passed in front of a "blind" beggar. The mendicant immediately took off his glasses and tagged along behind, maneuvering to keep this vision between the sun and himself. Lives there a man who hasn't indulged in the same sport?

With the coming of summer, at least some women would rebel against the many pounds of clothing in which propriety demanded that they sheathe themselves while bathing. In Chicago a startled policeman could hardly believe his eyes when he saw a woman slip off her bathing skirt and go into the lake clad in bloomers only—plus, of course, long stockings and baggy blouse. When she emerged he arrested her on a charge of disorderly conduct. The next day a sensible judge held that a bloomer bathing suit was both proper and legal, and dismissed the case. (A newspaper photograph suggests that the immodest bather's offense was against esthetics rather than decency. As nearly as one can tell, she was in her late fifties and weighed close to 200 pounds.)

In all the furor Paul Poiret, the French couturier, made the most sense. "The American woman is the best constructed creature in the world," he said in an interview in New York. "If her Parisian sister had such a form, there would be a new gown invented every day. It is unnecessary to wear a corset if properly gowned. The American is neither too fat nor too big around the hips to dispense with corsets. . . . The world criticized the tight skirt on its first appearance. Women couldn't walk in it. Naturally the slit, allowing her freedom, developed."

"Morality or immorality in dress," Poiret concluded, "—I know nothing of it."

Footnote on fashion history: J. B. Sheehan, president of the Chicago Retail Shoe Dealers' Association, declared that Chicago women had the best feet in the world, though large. On the average they wore a size 5B shoe as opposed to size 4½ for women of other large cities. (One wonders whether Mr. Sheehan had the measurements of the several hundred thousand Chicago women from Germany, Poland, and Bohemia, mostly of peasant origin.)

New music, new dances aroused the guardians of morality no less than new fashions.

Irving Berlin seems to have started it all with "Alexander's Rag Time Band," published in 1911. Here was a new kind of music, with a beat and accent radically different from such sentimental waltzes and ballads as "All Alone," "Somewhere a Voice is Calling," "Till the Sands of the Desert Grow Cold," and "Good-night Ladies," which all came out in the same year.

Nor was it only a matter of beat and tempo. The mood was different, titles were brash and sometimes cheap, the lyrics faintly suggestive. Composers followed Berlin's lead with "Oh! You Beautiful Doll," and "The Gaby Glide."

"Too Much Mustard" crossed the Atlantic from London.

In 1912 "Hitchy Koo," "You're My Baby," "When the Midnight Choo-Choo Leaves for Alabam' " (another Berlin production), "Here Comes My Daddy Now—Oh Pop-Oh Pop-Oh" and other similar tunes challenged such songs in the traditional, respected pattern as "Moonlight Bay" and "When Irish Eyes Are Smiling." While the new music by no means vanquished the old, it proved to be no passing fad.

Ragtime stirred the blood, set feet to tapping. This music called for dancing. But how could one go through the steps of the waltz, or even the two-step, to "You're a Great Big Blue Eyed Baby" or "He'd Have to Get Under—Get Out and Get Under to Fix Up His Automobile"? New dances met the need: the tango and the maxixe through importation from South America; the one-step, the turkey-trot, the grizzly bear, and the bunny hug by a kind of spontaneous combustion. All had two features in common: the partners held each other in a close embrace, and they moved about the floor with a celerity suggesting abandon.

Conservatives were shocked, but by the beginning of 1913 they could do little more than deplore the increase in sexual license that they were sure would follow. These dances weren't "new," the New York *Sun* commented editorially: they were a reversion to "the grossest practices of savage man" which had been preserved through the ages "by the habitués of low resorts, by strumpets and their patrons." They had never lost their appeal to the worst instincts of the profligate and the debased. "That . . . persons of respectable antecedents have injudiciously endured their introduction in places where decorum guards chastity has not changed their nature or obscured their menace."

Commenting on this editorial the Rev. Father William A. Brothers of Montclair, New Jersey, declared that "indulgence in the turkey trot, the tango, and other objectionable modern dances is as much a violation of the seventh commandment as adultery." Father Brothers admitted that he had not seen any of the dances, but he knew from what others had told him that they were indecent.

Highly vocal disapproval would continue throughout the year. In October, Dr. Melbourne P. Boynton of the Lexington Avenue Baptist Church, Chicago, denounced modern dancing as "muck-making, maiden-murdering, man-destroying." Anyone who indulged in this tangling of arms and legs, this dipping and darting, this open unashamed hugging would certainly move on to what he ambiguously described as "more disgusting lengths." Dr. Jenkin Lloyd Jones of All Souls Church (Unitarian), also of Chicago, bitterly deplored "the shivering souls who in decolleté dresses and swallow-tailed elegancies will chase after pleasure, trying to make respectable the tango and to justify by the sophistries of wealth those pleasures that had their origin on the low levels of lust and greed."

Defenders were few and discreet. In New York Miss Florence Walton, the partner of the dancer Maurice, contended that the maxixe was shocking only when danced "in certain ways." At one point in the dance the man raised his partner from the floor on his knee—a step which many observers found charged with moral significance. In this connection Miss Walton observed: "Every woman who weighs more than 130 pounds may consider herself safe from the temptations of the maxixe." To Maurice, the bad reputation of the dance came from the manner in which it was performed in Paris. The French made every dance suggestive, but Americans could be trusted to indulge in the pastime with propriety.

The doubters and the damners remained unconvinced. In November the *Ladies' Home Journal*, pillar of the home, still contended that all "careful-thinking and clean-minded people" could only regret the dance mania that was sweeping the country. The new dances were inexcusable in any society having regard for proper conduct.

A better index to reality was found in Chicago. There, in the winter of 1912-13, the committee in charge of the Assembly Balls, the outstanding social events of the season, had announced that only the waltz and the two-step would be permitted. Those who attended the first ball waited until supper was served and then commenced to tango and turkey trot. The committee was helpless.

In the following fall Mr. and Mrs. Arthur Meeker, social arbiters of the city, gave the largest party of the year at the Blackstone Hotel. The young people present danced the tango and the maxixe all evening while the host and hostess looked on benignly. And at 1:30 in the morning the popular dance team of Vernon and Irene Castle demonstrated the "Castle Walk."

(The big cities capitulated to the new dances in a hurry. In the smaller towns the case was different. In the winter of 1913-14 I took my first—and last—dancing lessons. At Hawkins' Dancing Academy in Mansfield, Ohio, then a city with a population of some 25,000, I stumbled through the waltz, the two-step—and the schottische!)

SPRING

In Omaha, Nebraska, Easter Sunday, March 23, began as a balmy spring day. From time to time clouds threatened showers and then dispersed, allowing the sun to warm the still-dead grass and the leafless trees. By mid-afternoon the fitful sunshine had been vanquished, and driving rain began to fall from a black sky. At 5:45, without warning a tornado struck the city. Missing the business section, the storm followed a diagonal course through the residential district, leveling 553 houses, eleven churches, and eight school buildings. Hospitals admitted 652 injured persons, the death toll was set at 150, property damage at $5,000,000. A few hours later the same storm smashed Terre Haute, Indiana, taking twenty lives and causing damage estimated at $1,000,000.

The Omaha tornado was no more than the prelude to disaster. On March 26 great scareheads marked the front pages of all the nation's daily newspapers. Dayton, Ohio, was covered with a seething flood from eight to twenty feet deep. Seventy thousand of the city's 116,000 inhabitants had been driven from their houses. A dozen fires burned out of the reach of firemen. Total darkness enveloped the city. Starvation threatened.

From Piqua, thirty miles north of Dayton on the Great Miami, came reports that a dam above the city had gone out and that 540 people had been drowned. Hamilton, on the Miami thirty miles below Dayton, reported that its reservoir had broken and that a thousand lives had been lost.

Columbus, on the Scioto, reported fearful loss of life and destruction. Delaware, on the Olentangy twenty miles north of Columbus, sent word that scores of people were clinging to tree tops and the roofs of houses. The city was appealing to Toledo and Cleveland for life-saving crews.

From Indiana, the news was almost as frightening. In Indianapolis, on the White River, 1,500 were said to be homeless. The fire department was helpless. Peru, on the Wabash, claimed property damage of $500,000 and placed its dead at 400. In Lafayette, on the same stream fifty miles to the southwest, the river had become a torrent two miles wide. Purdue University was isolated from the rest of the city. At Fort Wayne, in the northern part of the state, the Maumee and St. Mary rivers had spread far beyond their banks. The city had no lights, and famine threatened.

On Sunday, March 23 (the day of the Omaha Tornado) about a half-inch of rain fell on southwestern Ohio and southern Indiana. The next day the rainfall increased to two and a half inches. That night the people of Dayton retired with the Miami eleven feet deep, seven feet below flood stage. During the night the river rose more than seven feet, and in the morning, while the inhabitants were going to work, the water came at them "all at once."

Long before the river reached its crest of twenty-nine feet on the night of Tuesday, March 25, it had broken through some levees, flowed over others. People saw it swirl around the street corner in front of their houses, and before they could realize what was happening, found themselves marooned in brick and wooden islands surrounded by torrents ten or fifteen feet deep. Something like this happened in every other town or city in the river valleys where the rains had fallen.

Governor Cox of Ohio immediately ordered out the entire National Guard of the state, and appealed to President Wilson for tents, rations, and physicians. By his estimate, 250,000 people lacked shelter. Wilson ordered the Secretary of War to extend all relief in his power, and supplies flowed toward the stricken districts.[1]

As in nearly all disasters, the initial reports contained many exaggerations. Dams and reservoirs had not gone out, and there had been no "walls" of water. The simple fact was that steady rains had saturated the river valleys, so that when the rains turned into deluges on Monday afternoon and evening, the streams overflowed their banks. In some places levees broke, but the levees were already useless.

At Dayton, for example, the levees could contain a flood of twenty-three feet, two feet above the highest crest the Miami had ever reached; but on Tuesday morning the Miami stood at twenty-nine feet. At Zanesville, in southeastern Ohio, where the Muskingum and Licking rivers meet in the center of the town, the water rose fifty-

[1] *I remember the flood of 1913 very vividly. Mansfield, Ohio, stands on high ground. But when I came home from school on the afternoon of March 25 a stream of water about two feet deep separated our house from the one next to it. An hour or two later our basement was flooded to ground level and of course the furnace was drowned. For several years afterward, every heavy rain filled me with apprehension.*

two feet above the low water mark, fifteen feet higher than any previous flood stage.

Nor was the loss of life as high as the first reports had it. Hundreds, not thousands, died: a few under a hundred at Dayton, about the same number at Columbus, perhaps another hundred in all the other stricken towns. But property damage—houses demolished, furniture and stocks of goods ruined, machinery made useless, roads and bridges that simply disappeared—ran into the hundreds of millions of dollars. No one would ever make an exact estimate.

At Dayton, the worst hit, the disaster was blunted by the heroic work of John H. Patterson and the employees of his National Cash Register Company, which occupied a huge complex of buildings on high ground. When the flood waters covered the city Patterson, who had just been sentenced to a jail term for violating the antitrust act, transformed his entire plant into a relief organization. Carpenters pounded a boat together every five minutes, employees manned each one as it was finished, and rescued hundreds from second story windows. A hospital was set up and staffed; dormitories cared for the homeless. Meals were prepared and served. A communications center was established to break Dayton's isolation. Patterson immediately became the city's hero, and the thought that the government would send such a man to prison infuriated the townspeople. One old man told a correspondent: "I carried a musket fifty years ago, and I'm ready to carry one again!"[1]

With the courage that disaster always seems to arouse, the people washed away the slime that covered their

---

[1] *Patterson never went to jail. His conviction was reversed on appeal.*

houses and possessions, took up their old lives, and soon showed a grim pride in the extent of the disaster. Their's was the biggest flood since Noah's, and that they would maintain against all comers!

On March 31, at 12:05 P.M., J. P. Morgan, two weeks short of his seventy-sixth birthday, died at the Grand Hotel in Rome.

In Europe as well as in the United States, it was generally conceded that death had removed the most powerful person in the world. As one paper put it: "Kings have died, conquerors have fallen, with less world concern than attended the dying of John Pierpont Morgan, a private citizen of one of the youngest nations." King Victor Emmanuel of Italy and Pope Pius X sent messages of condolence. Elbert H. Gary, head of the United States Steel Corporation, called Morgan the greatest man of the age. To Andrew Carnegie he was the world's foremost financial magnate. Frank A. Vanderlip, president of the National City Bank of New York, asserted that "no man has ever been more closely, or more honorably, or more patriotically identified with the growth and progress of this country."

There could be no question about Morgan's power. Early in his career he had taken control of the Albany and Susquehanna Railroad from the two great "robber barons," Jay Gould and Jim Fisk. Through his own J. P. Morgan and Company he had reorganized one railroad after another in the 1880's and 1890's. In all his reorganizations he sought not only to reduce wasteful competition, but also to establish reasonable and stable rates for the benefit of the country. He had put together the United States Steel Corporation and the International Harvester Company. Twice he had come to the rescue of the government: in 1895, when he formed a syndicate to lend the hard-pressed Treasury $65,000,000 in gold; again in 1907 when, with deposits from the Treasury, he shored up shaky banks and financial institutions whose failure would have transformed the short-lived panic of that year into a financial debacle. In himself he personified the concentration of economic power that was a principal target of the New Freedom.

The people generally sensed that Morgan had other attributes than great wealth. His faith in the industrial and commercial future of the United States was unlimited. His integrity was beyond reproach, his judgment unquestioned. His power might have been too great to be vested in one man, but millions had no fear as long as that man was J. P. Morgan.

There was general agreement that the death of Morgan meant the end of an era. The opportunities he enjoyed would never again be offered. Government regulation and the decentralization of the banking system would prevent any man or group of men, no matter how able, from attaining his position of dominance. Even *The Iron Age,* considered by many a Morgan mouthpiece, said of his death: "It marks a transition."

The terms of Morgan's will were awaited with interest. How rich had he been, and what would become of his fortune? On April 14 curiosity was satisfied. The principal bequests were:

$9,000,000 to his three daughters
$2,300,000 to other relatives
$1,750,000 to friends
$ 450,000 to servants
$ 100,000 a year to his wife
$ 500,000 to St. George's Protestant Episcopal Church of New York
$ 600,000 to other churches

The residue of the estate, estimated no more closely than somewhere between $100,000,000 and $200,000,000, went to his son, J. P. Morgan, Jr. The son was also to receive his father's fabulous art collection, to dispose of it in such a way as to make it "permanently available for the instruction and pleasure of the American people."

On the following Sunday ministers all over the country took as their text the first paragraph of Morgan's will: "I commit my soul into the hands of my Saviour in full confidence that having redeemed it and washed it in his most precious blood he will present it faultless before the throne of my heavenly Father; and I entreat my children to maintain and defend, at all hazard and at any cost of personal sacrifice, the blessed doctrine of the complete atonement for sin through the blood of Jesus Christ, once offered, and through that alone."

The Theatre, a magazine of the stage, took a realistic look at the motion picture in its issue for April, 1913. No one could deny that the popularity of this form of entertainment, introduced commercially only a few years earlier, was increasing by leaps and bounds. Every day at least half-a-million Americans attended motion picture shows and spent $500,000 at the box office. Another half-million persons were engaged, in one way or another, in the business, which represented an investment of at least $200,000,000. Two thousand motion picture houses were in operation in the country, and their number was increasing at the rate of fifty a week.

Why this great surge of popularity? Principally, *The Theatre* explained, because the movies were cheap. The early nickelodeons were passing from the scene, but the ten-cent admission, now becoming prevalent, could not be considered onerous. Besides, the pictures made little demand upon intelligence. Many were either childish in plot or melodramatically lurid, and the "comedies" were triumphs of trash. Acting, if it could be called that, was crudely exaggerated. A few good actors had gone into the movies but the average player was hopelessly inept.

The Nation, in an article entitled "A Democrat Art," found an additional reason for the popularity of motion pictures. They conveyed a greater degree of realism than any stage production could possibly achieve. Action took place in real deserts, in real forests, on real oceans. "The heroine walks out of a very actual cottage, down actual steps, and takes a perfectly authentic trolley car to a real department store. The audience knows that these things and the trees, rocks, bridges, boats, and guns are absolutely true to life, because it has often seen the man with the camera at work. To watch one of these exhibitions is like seeing an animated popular magazine without the labor of turning the pages."

Yet, *The Theatre* recognized, the movies had already become a gold mine to a fortunate, far-seeing few. Only eight years earlier Marcus Loew had induced Adolph Zukor to give up his furrier's shop in Manhattan and buy an interest in a penny arcade. The pennies poured in, the partners bought more arcades, then small motion picture shows. By 1913 they had become millionaires.

The Theatre saw a portent in the experience of the Bijou Dream Theatre in Boston. (What town or city didn't have a Bijou in 1913? And how many of the patrons knew what the name meant?) When Mrs. E. H. Clement, wife of a retired editor of the Boston *Transcript,* took over the Bijou Dream in 1908 she found it operating along accepted lines: one-reel films of the trashiest order, a tinny piano accompanying illustrated songs thrown on the screen, and a travel lecture which all except the hardiest patrons accepted as a signal to get out. Mrs. Clement made a real effort to obtain pictures of higher quality, bought a good piano and kept it in tune, forbade the pianist to play ragtime, and put on an "amateur night" for aspiring singers once a week. Before long she introduced folk dances and one-act plays.

"Do the masses appreciate the high-class show that you provide?" *The Theatre* editor asked her. She replied that she had never advertised, and that the "Standing Room Only" sign hung at the box office several times each day.

In truth, the movies were changing, though the industry would not follow in the direction indicated by Mrs. Clement's experience. Better actors in better, longer vehicles would mark the road to future success.

As 1913 opened, the roster of movie actors included Norma Tallmadge, Tom Mix, Florence Lawrence, Clara

Kimball Young, Mary Pickford, Maurice Costello, Wallace Reid, Francis X. Bushman, Lionel Barrymore, and Mabel Normand, although most of them had worked only a year or two in the new medium. Few were known to the public. Some established actors insisted upon anonymity, fearing that their standing in the theater would be jeopardized, but generally the suppression of names was a device of the studios to keep the players from feeling too important, asking for more money, and demanding better working conditions.

But by 1913 "stars" were being featured. Mary Pickford, then twenty years old, came into her own with Zukor's Famous Players, appearing in three major pictures: "A Good Little Devil," "In the Bishop's Carriage," and "Caprice." Biograph developed the movies' first authentic comic, John Bunny. And at the very end of the year a young English actor, Charles Chaplin, who had been touring the United States with a pantomime company, joined Keystone. The "star" had, in fact, become firmly enough established that *The Motion Picture Story Magazine* decided to repeat the popularity contest it had inaugurated the preceding year. The winners, announced in October, were Romaine Fielding, Earle Williams, Warren Kerrigan, Alice Joyce, and Carlyle Blackwell.

The year saw the real beginning of "features." Heretofore most pictures, even such book-length stories as "A Tale of Two Cities" and "The Three Musketeers," had been filmed on one or two reels of 1,000 feet. In 1913 George Kleine imported "Quo Vadis?" from Italy. On eight reels, it was the longest film yet shown in the United States and ran for twenty-two weeks in New York at a one-dollar top, a price as unprecedented as its length.

Other imported features popular, even at advanced prices, were "The Last Days of Pompeii," "Les Miserables," and "Shylock." In the United States D. W. Griffith produced his first spectacle, "Judith of Bethulia."

One other innovation, the serial, made its appearance in the last month of the year. The first one was "The Adventures of Kathlyn," with Kathlyn Williams. The idea originated with a *Chicago Tribune* promotion man, who guessed that chapters of the story, appearing concurrently with installments in the motion picture houses, would boost circulation. He guessed right: the *Tribune's* circulation is said to have gone up ten per cent.

(My own clear recollection of the movies begins with the serial: specifically, with Pearl White in "The Perils of Pauline," first shown in 1914. I saw many installments in a "theater" which must have been typical of most of the movie houses of the time: a converted storeroom with aisles at both sides and one in the center. If it differed at all from others the difference lay in the fact that the ventilation was so bad that every few minutes the proprietor made a trip down the aisles pumping a perfume atomizer.)

Early in April the President let it be known that on the 8th he would appear before Congress in person and deliver his message on tariff revision. Not since the days of Thomas Jefferson, who had discontinued the practice because he thought it smacked too much of monarchical procedures, had a President been bold enough to break precedent. Several members of the Cabinet doubted the wisdom of the innovation, while in the Senate members of Wilson's own party expressed strong disapproval. The President, convinced that personal appearance was "the most simple and natural way" to appeal to the Congress, was undeterred.

Downward revision of the tariff was a cardinal point in the Democratic platform and in Wilson's own program. He had listed it as the first of his objectives in his inaugural address. He had said, in *The New Freedom,* that "every business question, in this country, comes back, sooner or later, to the question of the tariff." There he had argued that high tariffs led to trusts and monopolies, and kept prices at an artificially high level. The "infant industries" which the tariff had originally been intended to encourage had grown old, gray—and timorous. "When I hear the argument of some of the biggest business men in this country, that if you took the 'protection' of the tariff off they would be overcome by the competition of the world, I ask where and when it happened that the boasted genius of America became afraid to go out into the open and compete with the world? Are we children, are we wards, are we still such puerile infants that we have to be fed out of a bottle?"

"We have come to recognize in the tariff as it is now constructed," he had written, "not a system of protection, but a system of favoritism, of privilege, too often granted secretly and by subterfuge, instead of openly and frankly and legitimately, and we have determined to put an end to the whole bad business. . . . We mean that our tariff legislation henceforth shall have as its object, not private profit, but the general public development and benefit."

A good majority of the people of the country agreed, and had agreed for some time. Taft had sensed the public demand and had called Congress into special session in the first month of his administration to provide for revision. The result—the Payne-Aldrich Act—left the protective structure practically unaltered, and kept tariff reform a very live issue.

When Wilson adjourned a Cabinet meeting at noon on April 8 and proceeded to the Capitol he knew that he had the country behind him. His departure from precedent had brought crowds to the House galleries. When the President entered the chamber the entire assemblage rose and applauded, though without warmth. Speaker Clark announced:

"I have the distinguished honor of introducing the President of the United States."

Further applause, which Wilson acknowledged with a bow.

He opened with a disarming apologia:

"Gentlemen of the Congress: I am very glad indeed to have this opportunity to address the two houses directly and to verify for myself the impression that the President of the United States is a person, not a mere department of the Government hailing Congress from some isolated island of jealous power, sending messages, not speaking naturally and with his own voice—that he is a human being trying to co-operate with other human beings in a common service. After this pleasant experience I shall feel quite normal in all our dealings with one another."

The address was simple, short, unadorned with memorable phrases. The whole country knew that tariff duties must be revised. The national economy had changed radically within a generation, but the tariff schedules remained what they were before the change began. And the sooner the revision the better so that the financial burden carried by the public would be lightened and business interests relieved from suspense.

The principles of revision were plain, the President continued. Privilege or artificial advantage must be abolished. Aside from duties laid on articles not produced in the United States, and duties on luxuries merely for the sake of revenue, the object henceforth must be "effective competition, the whetting of American wits by contest with the wits of the rest of the world."

"We are called upon to render the country a great service in more matters than one," the President reminded his auditors, yet it was necessary to begin with the tariff. "I will urge nothing upon you now at the opening of your session which can obscure that first object or divert our energies from that clearly defined duty. . . .

"I sincerely thank you for your courtesy."

Prolonged applause, real applause, greeted the conclusion. The country applauded, too. Some dissented, but most people saw Wilson's crisp message, and his straightforward personal presentation of it, as something bold, free, and refreshing.

The President was delighted with the reception he had been accorded. On the drive back to the White House Mrs. Wilson remarked that Theodore Roosevelt would undoubtedly have done the same thing if he had thought of it. Wilson smiled. "Yes," he replied, "I think I put one over on Teddy."

The following morning Wilson broke precedent again by appearing in the President's room of the Senate for a conference with the members of the Finance Committee, which would have the tariff bill in charge.

Wilson knew well enough that as a practical matter, tariff reform would not be easy. All Democrats favored lower rates, but Senators and Representatives from New England could be counted on to oppose the removal of duties on shoes, those from Colorado would fight against free sugar, North Carolinians would decry any attempt to reduce the rates on textiles. And so on over the country.

Representative Oscar W. Underwood, chairman of the House Committee on Ways and Means, had spent months on a new bill. On March 17 he sent a draft to the White House. Wilson was not satisfied. While the bill called for drastic reductions in the rates on manufactured articles, it provided for duties on all farm products, retained protection for sugar and leather boots and shoes, and imposed a 15 per cent duty on raw wool.

On April 1 Wilson called Underwood to the White House and issued an ultimatum. The tariff bill must be rewritten to provide for free food, sugar, leather, and wool. If it weren't, he would veto it, and there would be no tariff legislation. The Ways and Means Committee gave in, and the bill which Underwood introduced immediately after Wilson's address on April 8 conformed to his wishes.

"It is an intelligent measure," the *New York World* commented. "It is not the product of intrigue and log rolling. It was bought with no corrupt contributions to a campaign fund. It was framed by the representatives of the people and not by the representatives of privileged interests."

Behind the scenes Democratic leaders struggled with

balky colleagues, and in the end obtained pledges from all except thirteen that they would be bound by a caucus rule obligating all members to support the bill in its entirety. On May 8 it passed the House by a vote of 281 to 139.

While house leaders lined up votes for the tariff bill, Wilson and his Cabinet were plagued by an international problem of the utmost delicacy and difficulty.

For several years the people of Washington and California, and particularly California, had become increasingly apprehensive about the Japanese who had settled inside their boundaries. These colonists from the Far East were prolific, industrious, and willing to put up with a lower standard of living than the whites. Even in California, where much the larger number of Japanese had settled, they numbered no more than 50,000, and made up only slightly more than 2 per cent of the population. The prospect of any large increase was small, for the Japanese government opposed emigration and had virtually stopped it by a "gentlemen's agreement" with the United States, effected in 1908. In 1913 Japanese farmers owned only 17,000 acres of farm land and leased another 150,000. Yet the people of California had persuaded themselves that these aliens constituted a deadly menace.

The California legislature met in March, 1913, determined to contain the "yellow peril." On the day after Wilson's inauguration the Japanese Ambassador, Viscount Chinda, called on the President to present the situation and express the concern of his government. The economic interests of Japanese nationals were involved. More important, the sensibilities of an exceptionally proud nation would be offended by any discriminatory legislation that might be passed.

Neither the President nor the Secretary of State knew much about the situation. Even after informing themselves, they failed to take California's attitude seriously or to recognize fully the gravity of its implications. They dropped a few gentle hints to California authorities, who, knowing the temper of their own people, paid no attention.

On April 15 the California legislature passed an alien land law which barred persons "ineligible to citizenship"—the Japanese were ineligible—from owning land. Viscount Chinda protested strenuously, and many groups in the United States appealed for fair play. In Japan, resentment mounted ominously.

Wilson could no longer keep out of the controversy. Through Bryan, he appealed to Governor Hiram W. Johnson of California. The President, Bryan said, recognized the right of the people of California to legislate as they chose, but he urged them to face the fact that a law such as that which had just been passed had an international character. Most earnestly he advised against the use of the words, "ineligible to citizenship." The governor paid no attention. (A few days earlier Wilson had written to former mayor James D. Phelan of San Francisco, one of the leading Democrats of the state: "I think I understand the gravity of the situation in California and I have never been inclined to criticize. I have only hoped that the doing of the thing might be so modulated and managed as to offend the susceptibilities of a friendly nation as little as possible.")

Wilson decided to send Bryan to Sacramento to make a personal appeal to the California legislators. Before the Secretary departed he gave his first state dinner, a testimonial of American affection and respect for the retiring British Ambassador, James Bryce. As soon as the guests were seated, Bryan rose. He related that when he had been offered the post of Secretary of State he had asked the President-elect whether acceptance of the office would require that he serve alcoholic liquors. He explained that he and Mrs. Bryan had always been "teetotalers," that their fathers had been teetotalers, and that they could not change their life-long habits without being false to their convictions. Wilson had told him to use his own judgment. Bryan hoped that he and Mrs. Bryan could show the warmth of their hospitality without serving wine.

The press had a field day, with British journals outdoing all others in cutting comments. That of the London *Daily Express* was typical:

"W. J. Bryan not only suffers for his principles and mortifies his flesh, as he has every right to do, but he insists that others should suffer and be mortified. This would be well enough if Mr. Bryan were a private citizen, but he is a minister of State, his guests are the diplomats of foreign embassies, and official invitations must be accepted."

But the most apt comment, as was so often the case in this year 1913, came from America's greatest philosopher, Mr. Dooley, presiding genius of a saloon on Chicago's "Archey" Road. To his faithful patron and ever attentive one-man audience, Hennessey, Mr. Dooley remarked:

"William Jennings Bryan . . . invited the foreign ambassadures to attend a dinner an' announced that he wud give thim on'y th' pure an' onferminted juice iv th' grape to dhrink. Th' ambassadures held a hurried meetin' an' cabled to their home governmints f'r insthructions. They were ordhered to attind in th' intherests iv peace, but th' Fr-rinch ambassadure resigned. At th' dinner th' sicrety iv state toasted peace in a dipper iv th' toothsome suds. In attimptin' to dhrink th' toast th' English ambassadure was attacked with a vilent coughin' spell an' was onable to respond, but was undherstud to say that there was worse ways of dyin' thin on th' field iv battle. In the mist iv an otherwise joyous dinner th' German ambassadure turned suddenly pale an' complained iv a horrible pain in th' stomach. He was able to lave the festive board an' be his own directions was assisted to a neighborin' ratskellar, where at 4 o'clock this mornin' he was restin' aisy."

Bryan arrived at Sacramento on April 28. Before an executive session of the legislature he pleaded for a measure that would not offend the Japanese. "Who is able to look into the future," he asked, "and tell us what it may mean to do that which may be regarded by the world as a declaration of inferiority, that which cannot but wound the pride of a nation that has made wonderful progress, a nation that stands among the powers of the world, a nation which is our friend and ought to remain our friend?"

The next day the California Senate passed a land bill differing from the original measure in only one respect.

Instead of prohibiting persons "ineligible to citizenship" from acquiring land in the state, it provided that all aliens "eligible to citizenship" could become landowners. Bryan warned that the Japanese would find the term "eligible to citizenship" as offensive as the earlier wording, but the legislators were unmoved. In this form the House passed the bill on May 3; Governor Johnson signed it two weeks later.

(Could it have been possible that Bryan lost whatever chance he had of influencing the wine-producing Californians with his first state dinner?)

As usual, Theodore Roosevelt knew better how to handle a situation than the administration. On May 2, after several telegrams to Governor Johnson of California, he expressed his views on the Japanese question to Henry White, who had spent almost thirty years in the diplomatic service of the United States:

"*Dear White:* I enclose you copies of my two last telegrams to Johnson. I shall not publish any of them, for this reason: the attitude of President Wilson and Mr. Bryan has been hopelessly weak, so as to render it quite impossible to stand up for them. Wilson's duty, according to my view, was perfectly clear. He should in the first place have asserted the power of the Federal Government to act as regards all treaties, and in the next place acknowledged its duty to safeguard California's interests. The Californian position is fundamentally right. The Japanese must not, as a class, own agricultural land. Moreover, they ought not to be here in any numbers either as small clerks and tradesmen, or as agricultural or industrial laborers. This was clearly understood under my agreement with them five years ago. With their usual fatuity, Taft and Knox surrendered the proper position by the treaty two years and a half ago. Their act in making this treaty was unpardonable, for they abandoned our right to keep out Japanese laborers. They excused themselves on the ground that they retained the right to abrogate the treaty. I need not point out to you that it is an infinitely more serious thing to abrogate a treaty in order to do what that treaty forbids than it is to exercise a right reserved under a treaty. One carries out a treaty; the other breaks it in order to do what the treaty forbids. Yet not only Taft and Knox, but the Californians themselves, paid no heed to this matter. . . . Wilson's position was rendered a little more difficult by this treaty of Taft's, but it was fundamentally the same as mine was, and his action should have been fundamentally like mine instead of the reverse. I told California that it was for the nation and not the state to act, but that I would adequately safeguard California's rights; and I did. That is, I asserted the national right, and I offered an adequate remedy. Wilson has told California that it was all right, but tried to coax it not to exercise its rights, and offered no adequate remedy. Under the circumstances all that Johnson could do was what he did, that is, pass the law demanded by the situation and try to see that it did not violate the treaty. Of course my view is that it is for the nation and not the State to see that the treaty is not violated. But when the President and the Secretary of State take the other view it is too much to expect that the Governor of the State affected will take the National view. Well! grape juice diplomacy under Wilson does not bid fair to be much better than dollar diplomacy under Taft."

Meanwhile, Viscount Chinda had filed a strong protest

with the State Department. The California land act was "essentially unfair and discriminatory," and obviously directed against the Japanese alone. It violated existing rights of Japanese subjects, was inconsistent with treaties in force between Japan and the United States, and was "opposed to the spirit and fundamental principles of amity and good understanding upon which the conventional relations of the two countries depend."

A war scare followed. The Joint Board of the Army and Navy urgently recommended that three gunboats in the Yangtze River be sent to Manila to aid in the defense of Corregidor. Admiral Bradley A. Fiske, Aid for Operations, informed Secretary Daniels that war was not only possible, "but even probable." Secretary Garrison, much excited, urged Daniels to join him in endorsing the Joint Board's recommendation. Daniels refused on the ground that the act would be provocative and of little practical value. The two secretaries took their disagreement to the President, who called a Cabinet meeting to discuss it the next day, May 16. Five members opposed the Joint Board's recommendation; four supported it. Wilson decided that the gunboats should remain where they were.

The members of the Joint Board proceeded to make fools of themselves. On May 17 they drew up a memorandum to Daniels protesting the President's decision and recommending that all destroyers and torpedo boats on the Pacific Coast be sent at once to Hawaii. They also requested the Secretary to present the document to the President.

Wilson blew up. Angrily he told Daniels: "After we talked this matter over in Cabinet and you and the Secretary of War informed these Navy and Army gentlemen that there was to be no movement now, they had no right to hold a meeting at all and discuss these matters. When a policy has been settled by the Administration, and when it is communicated to the Joint Board, they have no right to be trying to force a different course and I wish you would say to them that if this should occur again, there will be no General or Joint Boards. They will be abolished."

Wilson also ordered the Joint Board not to meet again without his permission, and he did not give his consent for more than two years.

The war scare vanished when Wilson told reporters that the idea of war was preposterous and made it plain that reports of American preparations were baseless. The Japanese government continued its protests and Bryan tried his best to mollify the offended nation. Neither party succeeded.

Arthur S. Link, Wilson's latest biographer, has an admirable summary of the Japanese impasse, especially relevant in the light of Little Rock and Oxford, Mississippi:

"We do not have to look far to discover the causes for this important failure of New Freedom diplomacy. There was Wilson's curiously narrow view of the federal government's authority, which prevented him from taking firm control of the controversy. There was Wilson's and Bryan's assumption that the California leaders would prove cooperative and that, in any event, professions of friendship would assuage the Japanese. There was Wilson's well-founded fear of violent controversy and defeat if he pressed for the ratification of a new treaty with Japan, which kept him from attempting to satisfy the reasonable wishes of the Imperial government. Above all, there was Wilson's own basic agreement, shared probably by a majority of Americans, with the anti-Japanese prejudices of the people of California, which led him and the State Department to try to evade the burden of Japan's protest by resorting to legalistic arguments. Whatever the causes of the failure, the consequences embittered Japanese-American relations for years to come."

While the California-Japan imbroglio stood at its worst, Bryan initiated a movement dear to his heart, and dear to the heart of the President as well.

Both men believed that the cause of world peace could be furthered by international agreements; both were convinced that the United States should take the lead in a movement to insure peace among nations. To be sure, arbitration treaties were in effect between some twenty-five countries, but they were burdened with so many reservations as to make them of doubtful practical value. Bryan decided on a fresh approach: a means of arresting developing controversies through a preliminary inquiry which would avoid the necessity of either arbitration or war. Wilson gave the plan his hearty support.

With the President's approval, Bryan met with the Senate Committee on Foreign Relations on April 23. The model treaty he laid before the committee called for (1) submission of all controversies to investigation, (2) a permanent international commission to make the investigation, (3) one year to be allowed for the investigation, during which parties to the controversy would refrain from hostilities, (4) reservation by each nation of the right to decide, after the report of the investigating commission, what action it would take. The members of the committee were favorably impressed, and approved the Secretary's proposal that he present the plan to all the representatives of foreign governments in Washington.

On the following day Bryan read "President Wilson's Peace Proposal" to the diplomatic corps. "Our nation desires to use its influence for the promotion of the world's peace," he told them, "and this plan is offered by the President with the hope that its acceptance by the nations will exert a large influence in this direction." The essence of the plan, he explained, was the feature requiring an investigation during which parties to a dispute would be obligated not to resort to hostilities. Bryan's proposals were promptly dubbed the "cooling-off treaties," on the assumption that in a year's time even collective tempers would cool and war would never be resorted to.

The "Peace Proposal" was given to the press, and Bryan spoke in its support at every opportunity. Some editors thought that one nation might sit through the cooling-off period in good faith while its adversary used it for such intensive preparations that it could throw diplomacy and arbitration overboard when the time came. To *The Army and Navy Journal* foreign jingoes might interpret the plan as evidence of national weakness. This same paper saw the timing as unfortunate:

"It may not only create in Japan a misinterpretation of the temper of the American people, but it is likely to show the people of California that the negotiations with Japan are being conducted by the State Department through the intermediary of a doctrinaire who is actuated more by devotion to his abstract theories of right than by a just estimate of the actual conditions confronting the Californians."

Most editors, however, were inclined to agree that Bryan had offered a concrete plan for the preservation of peace and that it deserved serious consideration. The Secretary himself faced the future with serene confidence. "I made up my mind before I accepted the office of Secretary of State that I would not take the office if I thought there was to be a war during my tenure. When I say this I am confident that I shall have no cause to change my view, for we know no cause today that cannot be settled better by reason than by war. I believe that there will be no war while I am Secretary of State, and I believe that there will be no war so long as I live, and I hope that we have seen the last great war."

The Secretary of State had imposing opinion on his side. Only recently (February 13) *The Independent* had given the title, "The Baseless Fear of War," to an article by Andrew Carnegie. The essence of Carnegie's argument was that the United States was secure behind its ocean barriers and needed neither a big standing army nor a navy larger than the one it possessed. To be sure, both Great Britain and Germany had navies larger than that of the United States, and France pressed closely for fourth place. As for Great Britain, "does any sensible man, naval and military officers excepted, fear war between the two parts of our speaking race?" Unthinkable, Carnegie answered. "Has there ever been danger of war between Germany and ourselves?" he asked. "Never has it been even imagined." Equally impossible, he concluded, was a conflict between the United States and France, two republics bound to each other by ties of friendship unstrained for almost a century and a half.

The whole movement to build up the army and navy could be charged to the professional military and naval officers. "Beware the expert," Carnegie warned, lifting an axiom from his experience in business. "A man's profession is his hobby," he continued; "therefore if generals are to decide how many soldiers we are to maintain, and admirals how many fifteen-million-dollar battleships we are to build to rust away, farewell to common sense, for there are no extremes to which men's hobbies may not lead them."

No nation, the old idealist concluded, had any cause for complaint against the United States. "The masses of the people in all civilized lands see in her the standard to which they fondly hope to attain and they love her. . . . We have no enemies, all nations are our friends, and we are friends of all."

Carnegie, Wilson, Bryan—all failed to mention that even then the armies of four Balkan states—Montenegro, Serbia, Bulgaria, and Greece—were locked in battle with the Turks, and that the imminent break-up of the Turkish Empire was bound to have the most serious repercussions. Not so David Starr Jordan, M.D., Ph.D., LL.D., president of Stanford University, whose article, "The Impossible War," *The Independent* published on February 27. Jordan recognized that the division of spoils, to come when the Balkan War ended, would tempt both Russia and Austria, two nations that were careless of their obligations, contemptuous of their neighbors, and beset by internal unrest. He admitted the possibility "that some half-crazed archduke or some harassed minister of state" could, "half-unknowing, give the signal for Europe's conflagration." But there would be no war.

Why not? The nations of Europe simply could not afford to fight. A war involving the five major powers of Europe, plus Romania and England, would see 21,200,000 men engaged. It would cost $55,000,000 a day. "The bankers will not find the money for such a fight, the industries of Europe will not maintain it, the statesmen cannot. So whatever the bluster or apparent provocation, it comes to the same thing at the end. There will be no general war until the masters direct the fighters to fight. The masters have much to gain, but vastly more to lose and their signal will not be given."

On July 15 *Life* asked the following question of a number of prominent citizens: "Will universal peace among the leading powers of the world come in the next one hundred years?"

Andrew Carnegie replied, predictably, that war would be abolished among civilized nations within ten years. The two most important influences in that direction were President Wilson and the Emperor of Germany, "who has reigned twenty-five years and kept the peace, his hands untainted by human blood; a great, a holy record." David Starr Jordan answered, also predictably, that great international wars were already at an end: "the world has not money enough to fight." From London Norman Angell, the English journalist who had written *The Great Illusion* (1910), asserted that permanent peace had already arrived. Germany, generally considered the most militant nation in the world, had not gone to war in forty years. The Balkan troubles were a lesson in point: "the more dangerous the situation got the less was the disposition that either nations or governments showed to war." John Mitchell, former president of the United Mine Workers of America, believed that in very much less than a century international peace would be firmly established. Organized labor throughout the world would take care of that. "As this movement . . . grows in strength and influence . . . as the doctrine of the brotherhood of man which it emphasizes finds lodgment in the hearts of all men, their determination to refuse to fight and kill their brothers will grow, until war, with its devastating power and brutalizing effect, shall have been banished from the earth."

Dr. Lyman Abbott, editor of *The Outlook,* was less certain. Wars could be expected until injustice ceased, and wars were not always as evil as the persistence of injustice. "The assassination of unarmed Armenians by Turks was more tragic than the Crimean War. The massacre of unarmed Jews by the Russians was more tragic than the Russo-Japanese War. The continuance of slavery would have been more tragic than the Civil War." Frederick Palmer, war correspondent and journalist, could imagine wars among the weaker nations. At the moment, he noted, war was ravaging the Balkans, China, Mexico, and Venezuela. "The hot-headed and weak can afford to fight," he observed, "but not the wise and strong. Whenever you find the highest civilization and universal conscription . . . peace rules." As for the future the United States, "unless it reforms its military policy along modern lines," would be at war before any two first-class European powers. The Honorable James Gustavus Whiteley, identified as "Unofficial representative of the President at the Congress of Diplomatic History at the Hague, 1898; Former Consul-General of the Congo Free State," contended that men would fight until human nature changed, but that such other diversions as auction bridge, the tango, and moving pictures were making the "game" less popular than it used to be.

The two men most reserved in their comments were the two men best equipped to speak: William Howard Taft and William Jennings Bryan. Progress in world affairs, Taft said in substance, came slowly. He believed that an increasing number of disputes would be settled by arbitration, but he would make no prediction as to the rate of progress. Bryan said simply that he believed the peace movement was gaining, and that all good citizens had an obligation to support it.

In a pre-season game with Philadelphia on April 9 the Brooklyn Dodgers dedicated their "magnificent new field and stand," Ebbets Field. With the weather cold and threatening only 12,000 people turned out. Philadelphia won, 1 to 0.

The season opened officially on April 10, although in some cities rain forced postponements until the 12th. In Washington President Wilson attended the opening game, swathed in a heavy overcoat with fur collar, and handed the ball to Manager Clark Griffith of the Senators.

Six teams took the field under new managers. At the

end of the 1912 season the most famous double-play combination in the history of the game—the Chicago Cubs' Tinker to Evers to Chance—had broken up. Tinker had signed as manager of the Cincinnati Reds, Evers took over the Cubs, and Chance, "the Peerless Leader," undertook to make a baseball team of New York's stumbling American Leaguers. Chance's contract was reputed to be the highest in the game: three years at an annual salary of $25,000 and five per cent of the profits. George Stallings with the Boston Red Sox, Miller Huggins with the St. Louis Cardinals, and Joe Birmingham with Cleveland, were also new at their jobs.

Late April, which saw the baseball season under way, the tariff bill moving toward passage in the House of Representatives, and tension between Japan and the United States mounting toward the breaking point, also witnessed the end of one of the bitterest and most protracted strikes in the country's history.

After 1900, West Virginia came up fast as a coal producing state. In 1912, the best year of the century, its mines yielded 66,786,000 tons of bituminous coal (one eighth of the national total) and gave employment to nearly 70,000 men. But only one district (Cabin Creek) of the coal producing area, which included parts of Boone, Raleigh, and Fayette counties near the Kanawha River in the southwestern part of the state, was unionized. Officials of the United Mine Workers were convinced that the future of the union depended on their ability to organize all the West Virginia miners, and the 80,000 other nonunion men who worked the shafts in Virginia, Kentucky, Tennessee, and Alabama. West Virginia operators, aware that theirs was a critical front, quietly brought in armed guards who put strangers entering the fields under close surveillance and now and then roughed up miners suspected of union sympathies.

The contract of the Cabin Creek miners expired April 1, 1912. The men asked for a wage increase but agreed to work pending a settlement. The operators accepted an increase in principle (with the amount unspecified) and then reversed themselves and insisted on putting into effect the lower wage rates prevailing in the unorganized field. The Cabin Creek men left the pits on April 20, demanding continued recognition of the union and a wage increase. Most of the nonunion miners of the coal-producing region followed their lead.

For the remainder of the year events in the West Virginia coal fields followed a sorry but well established pattern. Miners and their families were evicted from company houses and set up tent colonies. Clashes with the mine guards, sometimes ending in fatalities, took place with increasing frequency. In one pitched battle on July 26, 1912, twelve men, mostly guards, lost their lives. The National Guard was called out and restored order, but as soon as the troops were withdrawn violence erupted again.

Early in September, 1912, Governor Glasscock proposed arbitration. The miners accepted. The operators refused on the ground that the United Mine Workers were trying to organize the West Virginia field not so much for the benefit of the miners as to quiet the employers in the unionized fields in Pennsylvania, Ohio, Indiana, and Illinois, who were complaining of West Virginia competition. Late in November an investigative commission which the governor had appointed three months earlier made its report. Union miners, it found, had been guilty of beating up many nonunion men. On the other hand, the commission condemned the use of private mine guards, overcharging at company stores, and the operators' denial of the right of the miners to elect checkweighmen. As far as wages and living conditions were concerned, West Virginia miners were as well off as those in the union fields.

The strike dragged into the new year, with the companies becoming increasingly obdurate, the miners ever more desperate. On February 7, 1913, a chartered Chesapeake and Ohio train, mounting a number of machine guns, headed toward a tent colony at Holy Grove. With lights dimmed, it panted softly to its destination, then stopped opposite the first line of tents. The gunners opened up. Miraculously, only one miner was killed; the wife of another was wounded.

Three days later the strikers retaliated. Heading toward Mucklow, they ran into a detachment of mine guards. In the ensuing battle sixteen men were killed. Again the National Guard was called out, martial law declared, and 125 miners were held for trial by military courts.

Thus matters stood when a new Governor, Henry D. Hatfield, took office. Sensing that everyone had had enough of bloodshed, hatred, loss of life and property, he tackled the strike immediately. Early in April a number of operators in the Paint Creek district, employing 4,000 men, settled with the union. On April 25 Hatfield issued an ultimatum to all parties: bring the strike to an end within thirty-six hours. In less than twelve hours both sides agreed to the terms he proposed: the right to organize, a nine-hour day, the right of the miners to trade in non-company stores if they chose, pay semimonthly instead of by the month, and rehiring of strikers without discrimination.

The settlement appeared to be an almost complete victory for the union. But the verdict of the public was less sweeping. A committee of the United States Senate, after an investigation lasting several months, called the operators' resort to armed guards indefensible. Yet it found at least an element of truth in the contention that the United Mine Workers had conspired to organize West Virginia for the relief of companies in the unionized states, and it laid at the door of the union most of the blame for disorder and violence.

To a sober economist, Leonard W. Hatch of the New York State Department of Labor, the violence, lawlessness, and bitterness of the strike presaged another Homestead or Cripple Creek, armed conflicts thought to have been safely interred in the past.

The month of May provided the American people with a diverting spectacle: the Roosevelt libel suit.

During the campaign of 1912 rumors circulated widely that the former President regularly drank to excess, and that he often spoke under the influence of liquor. He decided that his duty to himself, his family, and the country required that he prove the falsity of the reports. He waited only for a responsible publication to print them. The occasion came in October, 1912, when the editor and publisher of *Iron Ore,* a weekly newspaper of Ishpeming, Michigan, charged that Roosevelt was guilty of habitual drunkenness and blasphemy, and that all his intimate friends knew it. He immediately filed suit for libel.

The case came on for trial in the circuit court at Marquette on May 26, 1913. Roosevelt was his own first witness. Before a jury of lumberjacks and miners he stated that at public dinners he sometimes drank a glass or two of champagne—on the average, perhaps, one glass a month —"and I do that in public." There was a fine bed of mint at the White House, and he might have drunk half a dozen mint juleps a year during his presidency. On his African hunting expedition a small supply of wines and liquors was included, with a bottle of brandy for his use as his physician prescribed. By the end of the trip he had consumed just seven ounces. He had drunk one glass of beer in his life and that had almost made him ill.

Some thirty witnesses followed the former President. They ranged from such celebrities as James R. Garfield, former Secretary of the Interior; Robert Bacon, former Secretary of State; and Lyman Abbott, editor-in-chief of *The Outlook,* to the butler at Oyster Bay and the White House barber. The burden of their testimony was the same: Roosevelt was extremely temperate in the use of intoxicants, and it would have been impossible for him to have been otherwise without their knowing it. Dr. J. B. Murphy and Dr. Arthur Dean Bevan of Chicago, who had attended Roosevelt after he had been shot late in the 1912 campaign, asserted that no alcoholic could have rallied as he had. The Associated Press summed it up in a sentence: "The colonel was trailed through every state in the Union and to Africa and back in an effort to discover if any one had ever seen him under the influence of liquor or ever had smelled liquor on his breath." No one had.

At the conclusion of the testimony, which took three days, George A. Newett, the editor who had made the charges, asked for permission to make a statement. During the trial he had concluded that so many highly reputable men could not misstate facts, nor could they be mistaken in regard to the former President's personal habits. He could only believe that those who had asserted that in their opinion Roosevelt had been intoxicated on certain occasions, and had even given depositions to that effect, were wrong. "In the face of the unqualified testimony of so many distinguished men who have been in position for years to know the truth," he concluded, "I am forced to the conclusion that I was mistaken."

Roosevelt followed the editor. He would ask the court to award only nominal damages. He had filed his suit for the sole purpose of dealing once and for all with slanders of long currency. "I have achieved my purpose, and I am content."

The court directed the jury to bring in a verdict for six cents, nominal damages in the state of Michigan.

Roosevelt, *The Outlook* commented, had performed "a real service to the country in bringing this libel suit and fighting it to a finish." *The Nation* agreed: the former President had given "a needed public lesson on the folly of believing, without evidence, the reports of private scandals in the lives of public men."

Mr. Dooley, a man of independent mind, saw in the verdict the end of an era. "In my day," he told Hennessy, "a pollytician was a baten man if th' story wint around that he was sildom seen dhrunk in public. His aim was to create an impressyon that he was a gay fellow, a jovyal toss pot, that thought nawthin' iv puttin' a gallon iv paint into him durin' an avenin's intertainment."

Who was the most unpopular President the country ever had? Mr. Dooley asked. Rutherford B. Hayes. Because he stole the office from Samuel J. Tilden? "No, sir, 'twas because whin people went up to the White House they got nawthin' to dhrink but sparklin' wahter, a bivridge, Hinnissy, that is nayether cheerin' nor ineebratin', but gives ye th' most inconvanient part of a deebauch, that is th' hiccups. Fr'm 6 o'clock, whin they set down to dinner, to 8:30, whin th' last southern congressman ran shriekin' down th' sthreet, this gr-reat but tactless man pumped his guests full iv imprisoned gas. An' whin his term expired he wint back where he come fr'm an' I niver heerd iv him again."

SUMMER

Shortly after noon on June 23, a sweltering day, President Wilson made his second appearance before both houses of Congress. The galleries were not as crowded as they had been on April 6, but the Cabinet members, Mrs. Wilson and two of her daughters, and most of the notables of Washington were present. The President's purpose was well known: to urge the passage of legislation reforming the nation's banking and currency systems.

The address he would deliver embodied principles worked out over months of behind-the-scenes maneuvering, and behind those months lay years of argument. Everyone agreed that the banking system was antiquated. Established in 1863 and 1864 under the stress of the Civil War and only slightly modified since then, it comprised some 7,000 banks operating under the general supervision of the Comptroller of the Currency, but without any central banking agency or any real co-ordination. The system was simply not suited to the great industrial and commercial nation which the United States had become.

The monetary system was even worse. The money of the country consisted of a hodgepodge of gold coins and gold certificates, greenbacks (unsecured notes issued during the Civil War), and national bank notes issued against government bonds. The supply of money was adequate for ordinary needs but too inflexible for seasonal demands. The Panic of 1907, caused almost entirely by the deficiencies of the currency system, offered a sharp lesson in the need for reform.

In 1908 the Republican Party had tackled the problem. A National Monetary Commission, headed by Senator Nelson W. Aldrich of Rhode Island—a man of the old guard, wealthy, conservative, and extremely able—worked at a solution for four years. The Commission's recommendations, handed to Congress in 1912, called for a central bank with fifteen branches and capital of at least $100,000,000, to be controlled by member banks in various sections of the country. The central bank, to be called the National Reserve Association, would carry a portion of the member banks' reserves, set discount rates, receive deposits of the federal government, and issue currency that would be the liability of the National Reserve Association rather than a direct government obligation. At the apex of the system the Aldrich plan provided for a board of directors composed of bankers and businessmen; administrative responsibility would be vested in a governing board consisting of government officials and private members.

By the time the Aldrich plan came before Congress the Democrats had taken control. Although the proposed system had the support of the banking and business interests, it was quietly shelved. Aldrich, now seventy-one, retired from the Senate, but with the satisfaction of knowing that his commission had so publicized the need for reform that action of some kind was inevitable.

Wilson and his colleagues faced the task of formulating an alternative to the Aldrich plan. The prime responsibility fell on Carter Glass of Virginia, chairman of the House Banking Committee, and the committee's adviser, H. Parker Willis. After conferences with Wilson, Glass came up with a bill to establish a federal reserve system of fifteen or more regional banks, owned and controlled by member banks, which would hold a portion of the reserves of member banks, perform other central banking functions, and issue currency secured by commercial assets and gold. A Federal Reserve Board, to be composed of six public members and three members to be chosen indirectly by the directors of the regional banks, would control the system.

When Glass presented a draft of his bill to Wilson on January 30, the President-elect was delighted. The two men decided on certain technical modifications which were all effected by the end of April. The bill, in what they hoped was final form, was handed to leading Democrats.

To the surprise of Glass and Wilson, it threatened to blow the party apart. The bill did not satisfy three requirements of the Democratic progressives: it did not provide for a controlling board made up exclusively of public members; it did not provide for government liability for the currency; and it did not insure the destruction of the Wall Street oligarchy of financial and industrial directorates fully exposed, so the objectors believed, by the Pujo investigation. Bryan expressed adamant opposition to the Glass bill, and the rumor spread that he would resign if it were made an administration measure. Senator Robert L. Owen of Oklahoma, chairman of the Senate Banking Committee, took the same position.

At this point McAdoo stepped in with a plan of his own. The details need not concern us; it served only to complicate an already delicate situation, and, under pressure, was soon withdrawn.

By mid-June, Wilson had come to a crisis. Banking and currency reform were essential to the success of his administration, yet he dared not force through a measure which, by splitting the party, would render it ineffective as an instrument of government. This the author of *Constitutional Government in the U. S.* knew as well as the most practical of practical politicians. On June 18 he called McAdoo, Glass, and Owen to a conference at the White House. The two questions to be decided, he told them, were control of the Federal Reserve Board and government obligation for the currency. He had not forgotten that he had approved the original Glass bill with its provision for banker representation on the board, but he had become convinced that in this decision he had been mistaken. Glass argued vehemently: a board consisting of public members only—"political" members—would be unjust and would arouse the implacable opposition of bankers the country over. With the latter contention Wilson agreed, but remained adamant. He insisted, with equal firmness, that the government must make itself responsible for federal reserve notes.

On the currency, Glass gave up, but a day or two later he led a delegation of Middle Western bankers who favored his bill as originally drawn to the White House. "The President was courteous and contained," Glass remembered. "These great bankers, arbiters for years of the country's credits, were grouped about the President's desk in the executive office adjoining the cabinet room. . . . President Wilson faced the group across the desk; and as these men drove home what seemed to me to be good reason after good reason for banker representation on the central board, I actually experienced a sense of regret that I had a part in subjecting Mr. Wilson to such an ordeal. When they had ended their arguments Mr. Wilson . . . said quietly:

" 'Will one of you gentlemen tell me in what civilized country of the earth there are important government boards of control on which private interests are represented?' "

A painful silence followed. Wilson broke it by asking:

"Which of you gentlemen thinks the railroads should select members of the Interstate Commerce Commission?"

With that interchange, Wilson sustained his position on the question of the composition of the Federal Reserve Board.

And so it was a President who had both cajoled and forced the leaders of his party to his support when he addressed Congress on June 23.

He began with an apology: he knew that "the heated season of the year"—a mild characterization of a Washington summer—was upon them all, and that a continuing session of Congress would be a burden on all members, and a threat to the health of some. Yet there were times when national necessity overrode personal convenience. "We are now in the presence of such an occasion," he asserted. "It is absolutely imperative that we should give the business men of this country a banking and currency system by means of which they can make use of the freedom of enterprise and of individual initiative which we are about to bestow upon them."

Without mentioning the report of the Pujo Committee which, after all, had only reinforced his own long-standing conclusions, he accepted its findings: "The tyrannies of business, big and little, lie within the field of credit. We know that. Shall we not act upon the knowledge? Do we not know how to act upon it? If a man can not make his assets available at pleasure, his assets of capacity and pleasure and resource, what satisfaction is it to him to see opportunity beckoning to him on every hand when others have the keys of credit in their pockets and treat them as all but their own private possession?"

In one terse paragraph the President summed up the principles which, by his decision, the legislation must embody. "We must have a currency, not rigid as now, but readily, elastically responsive to sound credit, the expanding and contracting credits of everyday transactions, the normal ebb and flow of personal and corporate dealings. Our banking laws must mobilize reserves; must not permit the concentration anywhere in a few hands of the monetary resources of the country or their use for speculative purposes in such volume as to hinder or impede or stand in the way of other more legitimate, more fruitful uses. And the control of the system of banking and of issues which our new laws are to set up must be public, not private, must be vested in the Government itself, so that the banks may be the instruments, not the masters, of business and of individual enterprise and initiative."

Three days after the President's address, Glass introduced the banking and currency bill in the House.

The conservative press, well informed in advance about

the principal features of the measure, had already begun its attack. On June 21 the *New York Times* had asserted editorially that the bill represented "the rooted dislike and distrust of banks and bankers" that had long been a moving force in the western wing of the Democratic party. "The measure goes to the very extreme in establishing absolute political control over the business of banking." The *New York Sun* was less restrained. "It is difficult to discuss with any degree of patience," it proclaimed on the same day, "this preposterous offspring of ignorance and unreason, but it cannot be passed over with the contempt it deserves. . . . The provision for a Government currency and an official board to exercise absolute control over the most important of banking functions is covered all over with the slime of Bryanism."

The financial interests of the East had declared war. The federal reserve act, in Wilson's form, would have a rough passage.

The country approached its national holiday, the Fourth of July, given especial significance this year because it would climax the fiftieth anniversary of the Battle of Gettysburg, fought on July 1–3, 1863. The three days in 1913 and the 4th, were to be devoted to a reunion, on the battlefield, of the survivors of the two armies which had clashed there. (No one paid much attention to the fact that the 4th was also the anniversary of the fall of Vicksburg, a Union victory at least as significant as Gettysburg.)

By June 30 the regular army officers in charge of the tent city which had been set up to accommodate the veterans estimated that 40,000 were already on the grounds. (Approximately 163,000 had been engaged in 1863.) Wet ground quickly churned into mud and heat so oppressive that it caused many prostrations could not depress the spirits of the participants. Veterans of Buford's division of Meade's army and Wheeler's division of Lee's, whose clash had marked the opening of the battle, held a reunion featured by the presence of six one-time Gettysburg school girls. When the gray-haired women quavered through "Rally Round the Flag, Boys," old Confederates wept as unabashedly as the former soldiers of the Union.

The formal ceremonies began on July 1 in a huge tent seating 15,000 men. Secretary of War Garrison delivered the address of the occasion and belabored the obvious: "The field of enmity has become the field of unity. . . . Thousands and tens of thousands of former foes are here gathered together in brotherly union. You who first met upon this field to vie with each other in doing hurt, the one to the other, now meet here to outvie each other in deeds of kindness and friendship and love. History holds no parallel."

(Earlier that day a solitary Confederate veteran had made the same speech in a single sentence. Encountering a group of men in blue he had offered his hand as he remarked: "I'm glad to meet up with you-all, boys.")

After Garrison, Governor John K. Tener of Pennsylvania held forth in the same vein. When he concluded, General Bennett H. Young, commander-in-chief of the United Confederate Veterans, rose and bowed with southern courtliness to the speaker.

"I can give you something that no one else can give you," he announced. "We will now give you the rebel yell."

Nine Confederate generals and a thousand former rebs let out a howl that reverberated through the camp.

Romance starred July 2; violence marred it.

Forty-six years earlier, as reporters picked up the story, John Goodwin, a Union veteran from New York, and Margaret Murphy of Chicago, had become engaged. The engagement was broken; each married someone else. Eventually they became widower and widow. A second engagement followed. Both came to Gettysburg to be married in the course of the reunion.

In the Gettysburg Hotel a Union veteran lost his temper when he heard several men speak slightingly of Abraham Lincoln. Rising to his feet, he came to the defense of the Civil War President. Someone pulled a knife, and in the fracas that followed, seven men were stabbed. When order prevailed again, the offended Union veteran who had started the affray had disappeared, presumably unscathed.

The high point of the reunion came on July 3, with a token re-enactment of Pickett's charge. The heat was too extreme for men in their seventies to attempt a realistic performance, so only 150 Confederates were assigned to march a quarter of a mile over the ground they had traversed in 1863. Even so, the going was hard: the ground was wet, the timothy high. Yet behind a band the plodding old men carried a faded Confederate flag, "its red field pierced with many holes, its crossbars dim, and its shaft colored with the sweat of many a man who died that it might fly high in that last desperate effort to pierce the Union lines."

Behind the low stone wall that had been the objective of

Pickett and Armistead a thin blue line had formed. Over their heads floated the white trefoil of the Second Corps, Army of the Potomac. As the Confederates approached, the men behind the wall cast off fifty years and sent up shouts of "Hurrah for the white trefoil!" "Clubs are trumps!" and "Forward the white trefoil!" But when the two lines came together the two banners were crossed and a third was broken out: The Stars and Stripes.[1]

Newspapermen and special correspondents of magazines exploited the sentimental possibilities of the reunion to the limit. A Union veteran was quoted:

"I was talking with my wife about comin', and we figured out it might be a pretty hard strain, but I said to her, 'This is most likely the last chance I'll have to do anything for the Union, and I'd like to do it fifty years from the time the Union was saved. It's going to mean something to all the younger generation to have us old fellows get together and show there isn't any hard feeling. It will take away the last excuse for the young people to cherish any sectional hatred.' "

A Virginian, standing at the Bloody Angle, described how he fell in Pickett's charge and how some Union soldier came along and saved his life. Just then a Pennsylvanian remarked to several Confederates around him: "It was right here that I gave one of your boys a drink of

---

[1] *Years ago the author heard, from an old newspaper man—he would have spurned the term "journalist"—that at this point several old Confederates in their exuberance jumped over the wall to embrace their former enemies. The Union response was instantaneous: "You sons-of-bitches, you didn't get over here in '63 and you ain't coming over now!" Fists flew, and only the presence of military police averted a riot. All my efforts to confirm the tale have failed, so I am forced to the conclusion that it is apocryphal. I wish it weren't.*

water, hauled him up on my back, and toted him to the hospital." The Virginian took the Pennsylvanian by the shoulder and looked hard at his face. "Why, good God, mister! You're the man that saved my life!"

Perhaps it was ironic that the star of the reunion should have been Major General Daniel E. Sickles, the only corps commander from either army able to be present. For four days Sickles held court, shaking hands with hundreds of veterans of both armies. At Gettysburg, fifty years earlier, by moving the III Corps to an exposed position in front of the Union line, he had very nearly lost the battle; for sixty years his private life had been notorious. But on this occasion a badge of valor—an empty trouser leg—atoned for all his deficiencies.

On the 4th Woodrow Wilson brought the reunion to its climax. Before 10,000 people—staff officers, governors, veterans—the President, himself a native of the South, delivered one of the most stirring speeches of his life.

"I need not tell you what the Battle of Gettysburg meant. These gallant men in blue and gray sit all about us here. Many of them met upon this ground in grim and deadly struggle. Upon these famous fields and hillsides their comrades died about them. In their presence it were an impertinence to discourse upon how the battle went, how it ended, what it signified! But fifty years have gone by since then, and I crave the privilege of speaking to you a few minutes of what those fifty years have meant. . . .

"They have meant peace and union and vigor, and the maturity and might of a great nation. How wholesome and healing the peace has been! . . .

"May we break camp now and be at ease? Are the forces that fight for the nation dispersed, disbanded, gone to their homes forgetful of the common cause? Are our forces disorganized, without constituted leaders and the might of men consciously united because we contend, not with armies, but with principalities and powers and wickedness in high places? . . .

"Here is the nation God has builded by our hands. What shall we do with it? Who stands ready to act again and always in the spirit of this day of reunion and hope and patriotic fervor? The day of our country's life has but broadened into morning. Do not put uniforms by. Put the harness of the present on. Lift your eyes to the great tracts of life yet to be conquered in the interest of righteous peace, of that prosperity which lies in a people's hearts and outlasts all wars and errors of men. Come, let us be comrades and soldiers yet to serve our fellow men in quiet counsel, where the blare of trumpets is neither heard nor heeded and where the things are done which make blessed the nations of the world in peace and righteousness and love."

Theodore Roosevelt did not intend to allow even the President of the United States to occupy the center of the national stage unchallenged. A meeting of the Progressive Party, held at Newport, Rhode Island, on July 2, gave the former President who had gone down to defeat in 1912 his forum.

Roosevelt spoke twice. July 2, Navy Day,[1] offered a

[1] *Since changed to October 27, Roosevelt's birthday.*

theme as congenial as any which he could have found. His first book, published in 1882, bore the title, *The Naval War of 1812;* he had served as Assistant Secretary of the Navy in McKinley's first administration; as President he had sent the fleet around the world on a practice cruise. To him Bryan's "two-battleship program," a vision of the day when the navy would be made up of the dreadnoughts *Friendship* and *Fellowship,* whose shells would carry good will and be projected by "the smokeless powder of love" was as dangerous as it was silly.

Roosevelt's two battleships a year, he soon made clear, would be armed with the most lethal weapons man could devise. Congressmen who voted against the big navy program were unfit to hold office, and by their opposition invited national disaster and humiliation.

"Let it be understood," he thundered, "that every man who votes to stop building up the navy or stop fortifying the Canal is voting to put us in a position where we cannot even resent insult, *let alone ourselves insult others with impunity.*[1] Let us remember that the policy of uniting the unbridled tongue and the unready hand is a policy of criminal folly. The most dangerous of all positions for any nation is to be opulent, aggressive, and unarmed."

In a slap at Bryan, Roosevelt characterized as wicked any resort to arbitration where national honor and national interest were concerned. The enforcement of the Monroe Doctrine, the protection and retention of the Canal Zone, Alaska, and the insular possessions of the

---

[1] *My italics. By this phrase Roosevelt defined the essential difference between himself and the moralist in the White House more clearly than that difference could have been defined in a thousand words. Wilson could never have said it.*

country, the determination of what aliens should be admitted and on what terms—all demanded power that could back words with deeds.

In the afternoon Roosevelt spoke on the goals of the Progressive Party, which he would not admit had been appropriated, with the consent of the nation, by the Democrats. Corporations and combinations in restraint of trade must be regulated by the federal government, and in this respect the Democratic program offered little hope. He had read *The New Freedom,* he said, but the book puzzled him. He assumed that there must be meaning in it, but all he could find was "the old license translated into terms of pleasant rhetoric."

The West Virginia coal strike offered an object lesson. At the root of the trouble was unregulated, cut-throat competition between operators, which resulted in starvation wages and dangerous working conditions. Even the courts had been corrupted, figuratively if not actually, since they had granted some of the worst injunctions—"the veriest travesty upon justice"—in the history of the country. The situation called for "the supervisory, regulatory, the controlling and directing power of the Government, precisely as the Progressives last year demanded."

"The Courts are the servants of the people," Roosevelt continued, "precisely as is true of all other public servants, legislative and executive alike. It is for the people and not the courts to say whether we shall have such laws in the interest of social and industrial justice, acts providing for cash payment in wages and abolishing these company stores."

In conclusion the speaker quoted, as he said, from Abraham Lincoln: "The people shall control both the legislatures and the courts, not to pervert the Constitution, but to overthrow those who themselves pervert the Constitution into an instrument for perpetuating injustice."

The author of several first-rate histories and a past president of the American Historical Association should have been more wary. The quotation cannot be found in Lincon's letters and papers.[1]

July 4 held interest for fight fans—and for a great many other Americans who hoped that the heavyweight championship of the world would soon change hands.

Since 1910 the title had been held by Jack Johnson, a Negro. This, a blow to white pride, was bad enough, but Johnson had made matters worse by his own conduct. He had married a white woman, an affront to millions. In the fall of 1912 his wife, then estranged, had killed herself. A few months later a federal judge in Chicago fined the fighter $1,000 and sentenced him to a year and a day in the penitentiary for violating the Mann Act: he had brought a woman, also white, from Ohio to Illinois for immoral purposes. Johnson posted bail and was given two weeks in which to prepare an appeal. Before that time expired he tried to skip off to Europe but was apprehended at Montreal and returned to the United States. (He was, after all, fairly conspicuous: very dark, six feet one inch tall, and 235 pounds in weight.) On his per-

[1] *Despite the brave words of its leaders, the Progressive Party was finished as an effective force. A remnant would nominate Roosevelt in 1916, but he immediately withdrew in favor of Charles Evans Hughes, the Republican candidate.*

formance outside the ring there was ground for hoping for his dethronement.

That hope—the "white hope"—centered in Jess Willard, a former farm boy from Kansas. Thirty years old in 1913, he had a five-year edge on Johnson. Six feet seven inches tall, he could outreach the Negro. Weights were about the same. Willard had been in the ring for only two years but he had not lost a match. And on July 4 he won another, defeating Al Williams at Reno, Nevada, by decision.[1]

The fourth of July, 1913, was notable in itself.

On July 4, 1908, in the eight representative cities of New York, Philadelphia, Boston, Cleveland, Cincinnati, Chicago, Kansas City, and Los Angeles, twenty-five people were killed and 670 injured.

On July 4, 1913, in those same cities, no one was killed and 143 were injured.

On July 4, 1912, in New York City alone 4,000 violators of the law prohibiting the unlicensed sale of fireworks were arrested.

On July 4, 1913, only 300 violators of the ordinance were apprehended.

Even in recent years hospitals were crowded with emergency cases on the national holiday; in 1913 they admitted few.

---

[1] *On April 5, 1915, at Havana, Cuba, Willard knocked out Johnson in the twenty-sixth round. Williard held the title until July 4, 1919, when he lost it to Jack Dempsey.*

"The new Fourth is worth a great many of the old," *The Outlook* commented.

Wilson was well aware that with the passage of the Underwood Tariff Bill by the House of Representatives he had won far less than half his battle. In the upper house the Democrats had a majority of only three, and no one knew how many would yield to local protectionist pressures.

On May 9, one day after the House had passed the Tariff bill, the measure was formally presented to the Senate. Before long, the President was confronted with evidence of the size of his problem. In the House, the lobbyists had lain low. What was the use of activity on their part? The Democrats had a safe majority, and passage of the bill was certain.

But the Senate, with its slim and uncertain majority, was different. Lobbyists moved into Washington on every train. Cane sugar planters, sugar beet growers and refiners, textile manufacturers, citrus fruit growers, sheep ranchers, shoe manufacturers, and dozens of other special interest groups sent in hundreds of representatives skilled in all the arts, and artifices, of persuasion.

Wilson was angry and disturbed. A brick couldn't be thrown, he said in a news conference, without hitting a lobbyist. He knew as well as anyone that a tariff lobby had never been defeated. In the administrations of Cleveland and Taft the lobby had prevented rate reductions of any consequence. If the lobby succeeded with the Underwood bill, what chance would there be for banking and currency reform, where the opposition would be even stronger? In the smooth, persuasive men to be found in every hotel lobby, at the clubs, even in private residences, the President saw a threat to his whole program of domestic legislation.

Wilson decided to attack. On May 26 he sent to the press a statement which, characteristically, he had framed without consulting anyone. "Washington has seldom seen so numerous, so industrious or so insidious a lobby," he asserted. "The newspapers are being filled with paid advertisements calculated to mislead the judgments of public men not only, but also the public opinion of the country itself. There is every evidence that money without limit is being spent to sustain this lobby and to create an appearance of a pressure of opinion antagonistic to some of the chief items of the Tariff bill."

It was of serious interest to the country, he continued, that the public should not be represented at Washington while "great bodies of astute men" sought to advance special privilege. Only public opinion could thwart their designs.

"The Government in all its branches," he concluded, "ought to be relieved from this intolerable burden and this constant interruption to the calm progress of debate."

In general, the public responded favorably, showering telegrams and letters of approval on the President. Republican Senators, however, were resentful. Wilson's statement implied that they were "approachable," and thus impugned their integrity. At their insistence a joint committee was appointed to ascertain whether, in fact, a lobby existed, and if it did exist, to bring to light its machinations. To add to the fun Senator James A. Reed of Missouri, Democrat, proposed that all Senators disclose property holdings or financial interests that might be affected by tariff legislation. No one dared protest.

For seven days, June 2 to June 9, a subcommittee headed by Senator Overman of North Carolina grilled his colleagues on their personal finances. The public followed the testimony with avid interest.

Senator Benjamin R. Tillman, Democrat, of South Carolina ("Pitchfork Ben") owned cotton-mill stock worth about $3,500, and produced cotton on his farms. He had owned about $2,000 worth of stock in an Oklahoma oil company for twelve years, but had only recently received a dividend from it.

Senator Elihu Root, Republican, of New York, former Secretary of State and one of his party's elder statesmen, owned 530 shares of National Lead Company preferred stock, 700 shares in the Smelter Securities Company, 220 shares in the Texas & Pacific Coal Company, and a 300-acre farm in central New York which produced crops listed in the tariff bill.

Senator John W. Weeks, Republican, Massachusetts—he would serve as Secretary of War under Harding and Coolidge—was the owner of 200 shares of the Hoosac Cotton Mills in Massachusetts. The company was recently reorganized after a failure, and had not yet paid a dividend. He also owned 75 shares of stock in the Scotia Mills in Rhode Island, and 50 shares of Strathmore Woolen Mills in Massachusetts. He operated "two or three" small farms in New Hampshire. "I have several life insurance policies in mutual companies," he concluded, "which some people think may be affected by the present bill."

Senator Henry A. DuPont, Republican, of Delaware, began his testimony by asserting that he, "like everyone else, was interested in the income-tax provision of the tariff bill." He owned several farms, but grew little produce for sale. He had 1,000 shares of stock in the Pennsylvania Steel Company, 1,000 shares in the Cambria Steel Company, and 1,000 shares in the National Biscuit Company.

Senator Albert B. Fall, Republican, New Mexico, turned out to be quite an operator. He ran about 10,000 head of sheep, from 1,200 to 1,500 head of cattle, and owned between 200 and 300 horses. He had coal mines in both the United States and Mexico, and bank stock worth between $10,000 and $15,000. He was also interested in the apple business.[1]

The lobby investigation produced little of value beyond its revelation of the financial interests of United States Senators. It proved, of course, that there was a lobby—which everyone knew already—but failed to reveal corruption or wrong-doing. But it did center attention on Washington, and made clear to Democratic Senators that they would find themselves in very hot water if they deserted their party on tariff reform.

---

[1] *Fall, after serving as Secretary of the Interior in Harding's administration, would become the only Cabinet member ever to go to jail for malfeasance in office. In 1921, almost destitute, he accepted a "loan" of $100,000 from Edward L. Doheny, who was interested in leasing the Elk Hills naval aid reserve, which had recently been transferred to Fall's department. As a result of the ensuing "Teapot Dome" investigation, Fall was eventually convicted of having accepted a bribe, sentenced to a year in jail and fined $100,000. He served time from July, 1931, to May, 1932.*

A Graduated Income Tax

For several years progressives in both parties had been urging the adoption of a federal income tax. Such a tax would meet the classic requirements: it would fall heaviest on those most able to bear it, and it would be difficult to evade.

An income tax had been resorted to during the Civil War, and had been in effect from 1862 to 1872. Another income tax bill, providing for a 2 per cent levy on incomes over $4,000, was passed in 1894 but declared unconstitutional a year later. The first step, therefore, had to be a constitutional amendment. In 1909 Taft, bowing to progressive pressure, recommended to Congress that it adopt the following amendment (the 16th), and send it to the states for action:

"The Congress shall have power to lay and collect taxes on incomes, from whatever source derived, without apportionment among the several states, and without regard to any census or enumeration."

Both houses accepted the recommendation almost immediately. Less than four years later the thirty-sixth state ratified the amendment. On February 25, 1913, Secretary of State Knox proclaimed it to be an integral part of the Constitution.

The adoption of the amendment was a windfall to the Democrats. An income tax, incorporated in their proposed tariff measure, would make up for the loss of revenue, estimated at $100,000,000, occasioned by lower rates. Cordell Hull, Representative from Tennessee, drafted the original proposal, which imposed a "normal" tax of 1 per cent on personal and corporation incomes over $4,000, with additional surtaxes of 1 per cent on incomes between $20,000 and $50,000, 2 per cent on incomes between $50,000 and $100,000, and 3 per cent on incomes over $100,000.

Beyond question, a large majority of the people of the country favored the imposition of the tax. Few families had incomes of more than $4,000 a year, and those that did could well afford to pay the small sums for which they would be liable. *The Nation* dissented. Taking a position out of character with its customary liberal attitude, it saw the income tax—any income tax—as a spur to public extravagance. Tariff duties had natural limits: step them up too high, and importations would stop. Real estate could bear only so large a burden. (The passage of fifty years has proved that the bearable load was far heavier than anyone imagined in 1913.) But there was no theoretical limit to an income tax. "It is possible for governments to increase repeatedly the rate of such a tax, without being stopped by its sudden non-productiveness." Therefore "the framers of appropriation bills, the projectors of increased national armaments, the log-rollers, and the pension-grabbers, may imagine themselves to have discovered the philosopher's stone."

The editorial appeared on April 17; two weeks later the magazine attacked again. The proposed $4,000 exemption was much too high. "A tax, general in its nature, yet such as to exempt thirty-nine men out of forty, offers a standing temptation to indefinite exploitation, not to speak of indefinite extravagance." The exemption should have been $2,000, and would have been except for the protests that figure would have aroused. The lower figure would have prevented what *The Nation* foresaw would become a habit—"the habit, on the part of almost the entire population of the country, of regarding a small class as the sole bearers of the burden of any fresh governmental expenditure, they themselves being interested only in its benefits."

No one—at least no one in authority—paid any attention to this journalistic Cassandra. Quite the contrary. In the Senate, Borah of Idaho and Bristow of Kansas tried—unsuccessfully—to raise the maximum rate to 10 per cent on incomes exceeding $90,000. LaFollette of Wisconsin tried for a 10 per cent tax on incomes above $100,000. In a Democratic caucus held late in August a compromise was effected: 7 per cent would be the maximum rate. Bryan endorsed it, and Wilson, then on vacation in New Hampshire, gave it his blessing. "My own opinion in the matter," the President said, "is that it is much safer to begin upon somewhat moderate lines." (One notes, with a grimace, the word "begin.")

"In the long run," Arthur Link has remarked, ". . . the income tax provision was the most important feature of the Underwood Act"—which seems to this author to be an egregious understatement.

During the summer it had become clear that the Senate would pass the tariff bill. The lobby investigation had blunted the weapons of the opposition, while the President had applied his own pressures, subtly but effectively. At a Democratic caucus on July 7, forty-seven of the forty-nine Senators present pledged themselves to vote for the bill.

Final action, delayed by the income tax provision, came on September 9. With the galleries crowded, and with many members of the House in attendance, forty-four Senators voted aye, thirty-seven nay.

Wilson immediately gave out a statement:

"A fight for the people and for free business, which has lasted a long generation through, has at last been won, handsomely and completely. A leadership and a steadfastness in council have been shown in both houses of which the Democratic party has reason to be very proud. There has been no weakness or confusion or drawing back. I am happy to have been connected with the Government of the nation at a time when such things could happen and to have worked in association with men who could do them."

Because of many Senate amendments, the bill had to go to a conference committee. The House approved the conference report on September 30, the Senate on October 2.

The President had won his first big legislative battle. To celebrate the victory, he invited some fifty party leaders, newspapermen, and friends to the White House on the evening of October 3, when he would sign the bill. He used two gold pens, one of which he handed to Representative Underwood, the other to Senator Simmons of North Carolina, who had had charge of the bill in the Senate. Then he made a short, informal speech:

"Gentlemen, I feel a very peculiar pleasure in what I have just done by way of taking part in the completion of a great piece of business. . . . It is hard to speak of these things without seeming to go off into campaign eloquence, but that is not my feeling. It is one very profound, a feeling of profound gratitude that, working with the splendid men who have carried this thing through with studious attention and doing justice all round, I should have had part in serving the people of this country as we have been striving to serve them ever since I can remember. . . .

"I was quoting the other day to some of my colleagues in the Senate those lines from Shakespeare's 'Henry V' which have always appealed to me: 'If it be a sin to covet honor, then am I the most offending soul alive.' And I am happy to say that I do not covet it for myself alone. I covet it with equal ardor for the men who are associated with me . . . and I covet it for the great party of which I am a member, because that party is not honorable unless it redeem its name and serve the people of the United States.

"So I feel tonight like a man who is lodging happily in the inn which lies halfway along the journey, and that in the morning, with a fresh impulse, we shall go the rest of the journey, and sleep at the journey's end like men with a quiet conscience, knowing that we have served our fellowmen, and have thereby tried to serve God."

In the third week of July an American tennis team consisting of H. H. Hackett, captain, Maurice E. McLoughlin, Richard Norris Williams II, and Wallace F. Johnson won the Davis Cup in play at Wimbledon, England. And the average citizen of the United States couldn't have cared less.

(That summer I was doing a boy's work in my father's grocery store. We went home, a mile distant, for lunch. We both had bicycles, but because of a fairly steep grade we had to walk about a third of the way. In a vacant lot half-way up the hill someone had recently built a tennis court, and whenever a game was in progress we stopped to watch for a few minutes. My father's comment was invariably the same. "LOVE fifteen! LOVE thirty!" he would snort. "What kind of a game is that!")

"A struggle that for bitterness and obstinacy has rarely been surpassed in American industrial history." Thus *The Outlook* characterized the strike of Paterson, New Jersey, silk workers that came to an end in the last week of July.

Paterson, a city of 125,000, had nearly 300 silk mills and dyeing plants—a fifth of the silk industry of the country. In 1912 the employers inaugurated the three- and four-loom system, under which each weaver was compelled to attend three or four looms instead of the customary two, and without increase in pay. The workers smoldered with resentment until late January, 1913, when many of the employees of the Henry Doherty Company, one of the largest firms, left their looms.

In this situation the I.W.W.—Industrial Workers of the World—saw its chance. Organized in 1905, the "one big union" had recruited no more than 100,000 members even though its dues were low and its methods direct. Goals that it made no effort to conceal—the destruction of capitalism, the taking over of all industry by the workers—

sent shivers through every businessman of the time.

I.W.W. organizers in Paterson knew that the silk workers had made at least two appeals to the American Federation of Labor to take action against the encroachment of the four-loom system. Nothing had happened. Winning adherents fast, the I.W.W. called a strike at the Doherty Company on February 1, and converted it into a strike throughout the industry on February 25. Eight thousand workers responded immediately, and within a week all 25,000 employees were idle. The dyers demanded a minimum wage of $12.00 a week; weavers wanted a return to the two-loom system and a 25 per cent increase in wages; ribbon workers called for the reinstatement of an earlier and higher piecework scale.

I.W.W. locals over the country sent money to Paterson. I.W.W. leaders—William D. ("Big Bill") Haywood, Elizabeth Gurley Flynn, Carlo Tresca, Joseph Ettor, Patrick Quinlan—headed for the city. Local authorities ordered them out. They refused to leave. Haywood was arrested, convicted of disorderly conduct, and sentenced to six months in jail. On appeal the conviction was reversed and the Paterson police were reprimanded, but they continued to harass other leaders and pickets. Even the right of assembly was denied, but the Socialist mayor of nearby Haledon came to the rescue of the strikers and invited them to hold their meetings there.

The I.W.W. quickly won the loyalty of the strikers. Within three months its membership jumped from 1,500 to 10,500. Haywood's claim that there was a red card in the home of every silk worker was no great exaggeration. Between 10,000 and 20,000 strikers and sympathizers turned out every week for the Sunday outdoor rally at

Haledon. Low dues helped: thirty cents a month without any initiation fee, while some of the craft unions affiliated with the A. F. of L. charged initiation fees as high as $25.00. The Sons of Italy, a benevolent society, furthered solidarity among the strikers. (Italians outnumbered all other nationalities.) When the strike was two months old John Golden, president of the United Textile Workers of America (A. F. of L.), tried to move in. The strikers refused even to listen to him.

Neither party to the dispute would entertain proposals that it be arbitrated. Neither, in sober fact, had anything to give. The workers could barely live on their wages, the employers could pay no more and survive. Pay rates at Paterson were higher than in any other silk manufacturing center in the country. Much of the silk was processed by "backyard" factories operated by owners and their families. No wage increase could be made to apply to these little plants, and they, with competitors in other states where wages were lower and labor laws more lax, would soon put the big operators out of business.

In the end, sheer poverty settled the strike. The strikers soon ran out of savings. The butchers and grocers and landlords who extended credit, as many did, went bankrupt with increasing frequency. The I.W.W. exhausted its limited resources. In June workers began to drift back to work. The drift gained momentum in July, and when the month ended nearly all those who had walked out twenty-two weeks earlier were back at work. They had gained nothing for the $5,000,000 they had lost in wages.

Thoughtful observers saw portents in the Paterson strike. Both sides were powerless in the grip of economic necessities. The workers had to have more money and work shorter hours if they were to live as decent human beings. The manufacturers had to resort to what we have come to call automation or they could not keep men and women employed even at the prevailing wages. Gregory Mason, writing in *The Outlook,* identified "indiscriminate and unregulated competition both within and among states" as the basic cause of conflict. "Both the manufacturers and their opponents in Paterson," he wrote, "say that they would welcome a Federal law fixing a standard of wages and hours of labor throughout the silk industry, if the time-worn states' rights bugaboo would not arise to block such a law. Certainly state co-operation in the establishment of uniform labor statutes is needed."

In the strike, the municipal authorities of Paterson demonstrated how not to deal with a labor disturbance. "The county jail," Gregory Mason wrote, "has been crowded with strikers sent there on charges of inciting to riot, unlawful assemblage, etc. In many cases the only offense of these prisoners has seemed to be their presence on the picket line or on the platform at strike meetings." How many arrests were made remains questionable. *The Outlook* placed the number at 1,473; Perlman and Taft, in their *History of Labor in the United States, 1896-1932,* settled on 2,338. Of these, 300 were held to the grand jury and 100 were sentenced to imprisonment, though few of the sentences were served. Beyond doubt, this widespread disregard of due process stiffened the determination of the strikers to hold out to the end.

Leonard W. Hatch, Chief Statistician of the New York State Department of Labor, reviewing the strike in *The American Year Book,* saw in it an indication that the industrial union, and particularly the I.W.W., would become increasingly important in the labor movement. The Paterson strikers cared nothing about the I.W.W.'s ultimate goal of putting the workers in control of the means of production. They simply wanted more money and better working conditions, but in the absence of aid from any other source they accepted I.W.W. leadership. So, Mr. Hatch concluded, an "increasing number of industrial communities made up, as at Paterson, largely of low-paid workers of foreign extraction, may be expected under economic pressure to offer quick acceptance of the leadership of champions holding revolutionary doctrines."

Mr. Hatch, like many economists before and since, was a poor prophet. The I.W.W. would never again conduct a major strike, and would soon become so insignificant that no one would worry about it.

On July 21, a warm bright day, the sewing machines hummed steadily in the Binghamton Clothing Factory at Binghamton, New York.

Local people regarded the factory as a model. Four stories high and built of brick, the walls, sixteen inches thick, had not shown a crack in twenty years. The hundred or more employees, mostly women, were well paid and happy in their work. Owners of the company had been quick to comply with fire regulations, and the building had passed an inspection only a few weeks earlier.

In mid-afternoon the fire alarm rang insistently. Most of the women on the third and fourth floors rose from their machines. Others remained at work—fire drills took time, and when one worked at piece rates, time meant money. Besides, they disliked appearing on the street in thin plain work dresses. Even when one of the women saw smoke emerging from a chute some were reluctant to leave: at a recent fire drill someone had suggested that a smudge would make the exercise more realistic.

The women who did start down the stairs saw at once that this was no safety drill. Between the first and second floors flames filled the stairwell. One girl related: "I ran down as many steps as I could, then threw my dress over my head and jumped over the fire. I felt myself falling, and it seemed as though I landed on a pile of girls. After that I must have lost consciousness."

Other women—the ones who had not responded promptly to the alarm—resorted to the outdoor fire escape, which did not extend below the second story. As the first of the women hesitated to jump those above them pushed, and soon a heap of bodies lay on the pavement. In twenty-three minutes from the time of the alarm the building collapsed. Of the 111 women who had been at work, fifty-eight were dead.

An investigation by the New York Committee of Safety established certain facts:

1. The building had only one stairway.
2. The single stairway was not enclosed and fireproofed.
3. The outdoor iron fire escape warped under heat and could not accommodate more than six or seven persons per floor.
4. Both stairway and fire escape could not have afforded a quick, safe means of exit to more than forty persons on the third and fourth floors, yet seventy women were at work on the fourth floor alone.

None of these deficiencies constituted an infraction of the state fire laws. Inis Weed, writing in *The Outlook,* observed:

"It took an Iroquois Theater fire to improve the safety of theaters. It took a *Titanic* disaster to improve the safety of vessels. It took a Newark fire and a Triangle fire to bring New York State's fire legislation to its present inefficiency. Now fifty-eight women have sacrificed their lives. By so doing they have proved the untruth of the statements made to the Legislature that human lives could not be destroyed by fire in low buildings. The present law was framed on this false assumption. Will the Legislature act to correct this fatal blunder?"

Domestic issues should have been enough in the hot summer of 1913, but they weren't. Mexico, as an international problem, flared up again.

Internally, the nation had not stopped simmering. In late March opponents of Huerta had demanded the restoration of constitutional government and had appointed Venustiano Carranza, Governor of the State of Coahuila, as leader of the movement to overthrow the tyrant in Mexico City. A few days later Carranza proclaimed himself provisional president. With "Pancho" Villa and Alvaro Obregon, Carranza controlled most of northern Mexico. In Morelos, southwest of the capital, Emiliano Zapata, a far more radical reformer than Carranza, held a sizable territory. Though in possession of the seat of government, Huerta could hardly claim that he had pacified the country.

American residents in Mexico representing extensive interests there were deeply disturbed by the situation. A continuing civil war, they saw clearly enough, would be disastrous. So far, Huerta had not disturbed them, but could he ever put down the forces against him? In doubt on this point, officers of several American corporations heavily involved in Mexico formulated a policy for Wilson's consideration. Recognize Huerta on condition that he hold an early election in the states which he controlled. Put pressure on Carranza to take the same step. Both factions should be made to agree in advance that they would support the president thus chosen.

Wilson was favorably impressed. But soon afterward the men responsible for the proposal changed their minds. Now they recommended that the United States should do no more than offer to mediate between the factions to the end that a fair national election be held to choose a president. Wilson agreed, and even embodied the new proposal in instructions to be sent to Harry Lane Wilson in Mexico City. Then he hesitated. Each passing day increased his distrust of the aggressively pro-Huerta American Ambassador, and made him increasingly aware of his own ignorance of conditions south of the Rio Grande.

Before taking any positive step, he decided, he must have more information. To obtain it from an unprejudiced source he decided to send a special envoy who would report to him directly. For the mission he chose a personal and political friend, William Bayard Hale, a clergyman turned editor and author who had written a campaign biography of Wilson and had compiled *The New Freedom*. That Hale had a claim to presidential preferment is obvious. That he had any knowledge or experience that could serve the President in a perplexing predicament is hard to see.

Hale left for Mexico in late May. His first report was written on June 3; others followed at short intervals until late August. Hale confirmed the low estimate of Huerta that Wilson had already formed. Hale soon became convinced that Huerta could not survive, and that if events in Mexico were allowed to run their course, the United States would have to occupy the country. Hale urged Wilson to demand the elimination of Huerta, the holding of free elections, and the formation of a new government. He was sure that if the United States made it plain that it was prepared to use force to obtain its demands, Huerta would yield.

Meanwhile, Wilson and Bryan had sent another emissary, one Reginald F. Del Valle, to northern Mexico to take Carranza's measure, but Del Valle proved to be so incompetent that he was abruptly recalled.

In the last two weeks of July Wilson and Bryan decided on a course of action. Their first move was to recall Harry Lane Wilson, ostensibly for consultation but actually to relieve him. Then they selected, on Bryan's recommendation, a former congressman and governor of Minnesota, John Lind, to go to Mexico as the President's personal representative. Lind's qualifications were as obscure as those of Hale, and again the country was surprised at Wilson's choice for a delicate diplomatic mission.

Lind set off on August 4 with instructions which Wilson himself had written. After a profession of friendship and a declaration that the United States desired only Mexico's welfare, the instructions read:

"The present situation in Mexico is incompatible with

the fulfillment of international relations on the part of Mexico, with the civilized development of Mexico herself, and with the maintenance of tolerable political and economic conditions in Central America. It is upon no common occasion, therefore, that the United States offers her counsel and assistance. All America cries out for a settlement.

"A satisfactory settlement seems to us to be conditioned on:

"(a) An immediate cessation of fighting throughout Mexico, a definite armistice solemnly entered into and scrupulously observed;

"(b) Security given for an early and free election in which all will agree to take part;

"(c) The consent of General Huerta to bind himself not to be a candidate for election as President of the Republic at this election; and

"(d) The agreement of all parties to abide by the results of the election and co-operate in the most loyal way in organizing and supporting the new administration."

Wilson, with incredible naiveté, had not consulted with the American Embassy in Mexico City, the Huerta government, the Constitutionalist leaders, or any representatives of foreign governments with interests in Mexico before releasing Lind's instructions to the press.

Huerta exploded. He would not receive Lind unless he bore credentials as ambassador—which of course he did not. Nevertheless, Lind did call on Gamboa, Huerta's foreign minister, and two days later, August 14, presented the American President's proposals. In succeeding conferences Lind put on pressure, warning that the United States might supply arms to the Constitutionalists (which so far it had refrained from doing), and might even use force to topple the provisional government. Finally he played his trump card: the United States would approve a large loan to the provisional government if Huerta would agree to hold a fair election and promise that he would not be a candidate for the presidency.

On August 26 Gamboa bluntly rejected all the American advances. "If even once," his note read, "we were to permit the counsels and advice (let us call them thus) of the United States of America, not only would we . . . forego our sovereignty but we would as well compromise for an indefinite future our destinies as a sovereign entity, and all the future elections for president would be submitted to the veto of any President of the United States of America."

That ended the Lind mission.

(About the same time an American journalist asked a little Mexican girl living in the United States whether she thought Uncle Sam should send an army to straighten out her unhappy homeland.

"No," she answered. "Why can't this big country let our little country born itself?")

On August 27, the day Lind left Mexico City for the United States, Wilson explained the Mexican policy of the administration to the Congress in joint session—and of course to the American people. The United States desired only to see peace restored in Mexico and an honest constitutional government set up there. Huerta had proved his incapacity, and "war and disorder, devastation and confusion" seemed inevitable if events ran their course. "It was only our duty at least to volunteer our good offices —to offer to assist, if we might, in effecting some arrangement which would bring relief and peace and set up a universally acknowledged political authority there."

But the provisional government had rejected the American proposals. What then? The United States could only await developments with patience. Americans living in Mexico would be urged to leave at once, while at the same time Mexican authorities would be warned that they would be held responsible for unavoidable American suffering and property loss. Export of arms or munitions of war to any part of the Republic would be forbidden.

Wilson closed with a prophecy: "The steady pressure of moral force will before many days break the barriers of pride and prejudice down, and we shall triumph as Mexico's friends sooner than we could triumph as her enemies—and how much more handsomely, with how much higher and finer satisfactions of conscience and of honor!"

Thus was announced the policy which newspapers promptly dubbed "watchful waiting"—a policy overwhelmingly approved by the American people. Perhaps their response would have been less enthusiastic had they known that Huerta and his ringleaders were delighted also. Nonintervention on the part of the United States would work to their benefit. The Carranzistas were landlocked; the provisional government controlled the seaports. It, and it alone, could import munitions from Europe and Japan.

"Watchful waiting," no matter how popular, would never solve the impasse between Mexico and the United States. The fundamental difficulty was a Scotch-Irish Presbyterian conscience that would accept no pragmatic solution. Nearly fifty years later Arthur Link, Wilson's biographer, wrote that the basic weakness of the New Freedom diplomacy was the naiveté of its premises. "Wilson and Bryan assumed that moral force controlled the relations of powers, that reason would prevail over ignorance and passion in the formation of public opinion, and that men and nations everywhere were automatically progressing toward an orderly and righteous international society. If these assumptions were true, then a combination of Christian love and moral suasion *would* suffice to solve all international problems."

But the assumptions weren't true. This Mr. Dooley recognized even before John Lind had given up his effort to lead Huerta and Gamboa along the path of peace, righteousness, and constitutional government.

"What's the throuble in Mexico?" the philosopher of Archer Road asked Hennessey, facing him on the other side of the bar. "Well, it's a difference of opinyon in th' Wilson fam'ly about th' kind iv people they ought to assocyate with. Hinnery Lane Wilson, him that is our ambassadure to Mexico but is soon to resoom th' practice iv law in Spokane, is a gr-reat diplomat, a good mixer, who takes th' wurruld as he finds it an' overlooks small faults in th' men that he likes. Afther Gin'ral Hurta had claned off his revolver an' put his bowie knife back in his pocket an' became prisidint iv Mexico, Hinnery, who felt a gr-reat fondness f'r th' gin'ral in spite iv th' nervous twitchin' in his pistol finger, thried to inthrojooce him to Doc Wilson. 'Doc,' says he, 'I want ye to shake hands with me frind Hurta. Ye two boys ought to know each other, bein' in th' same line.' Thin he whispered to Doc: 'Don't pay any attintion to his face. It is not aisy to look at, but he has a heart iv goold. He's a man iv high sthrung timp'ramint, a thrifle careless iv human life at times an' somewhat given to threachery, but who iv us is without faults? Besides I've already reco'nized him, an' ye might just as well get into line,' he says. But Doc Wilson has become partiklar about his friends since he got to be prisident. He said he'd be somethin'—or other—if he'd reco-'nize a prisidint that got his certifycate iv office fr'm th' coroner. If he wanted to hook up with that school iv statesmanship he'd ask Gyp th' Blood to come down to Washin'ton an' visit with him. 'This here spoort iv killin' prisidints has gone far enough,' he says. 'I don't sympathize with it in th' laste. It is a bad precidint an' I'll do nawthin' in anny way to establish it.' "

With the Mexican situation on the front page of every newspaper, the Secretary of State took the spotlight at home. For years Bryan had been a star lecturer on the Chautauqua circuit. In July he made his first appearance of the new season. Editors went into action with gusto: international problems demanded the entire time and attention of the Secretary of State, and besides, Chautauqua performances were incompatible with the dignity of Bryan's office.

Bryan, stung by the criticism, explained his position in the course of a lecture at Hendersonville, North Carolina, on July 13. He could not live on his salary of $12,000 a year. Insurance premiums and obligations to church, charity, and education took $7,000 annually. This sum he had to earn on the platform. There was nothing dishonorable about lecturing for fees, and he saw no reason to be ashamed of sharing his experience and thoughts with the American people. He would keep an engagement to appear at Mountain Lake Park, Maryland, on July 17, and later in the summer he would tour the Middle West for six weeks.

The next day Senator Bristow of Kansas, a Republican, introduced a resolution calling on the President to advise the Senate on what would be a proper salary "to enable the present Secretary of State to live with comfort, and to enable him to give his time to the discharge of his public duties." While the Republicans laughed, the Democratic majority tabled the resolution.

Bryan, stung again, issued a public statement. For seventeen years he had earned, from speaking and writing, an income large enough to enable him to pay all living expenses and save $10,000 a year. When he accepted his present office he was willing to forego his savings program, but he had to lecture often enough to bring his income up to his living expenses. He was convinced, moreover, that his lectures were good for the country.

In the weeks that followed newspapers and magazines devoted almost as much space to Bryan's Chautauqua performances as to affairs in Mexico. Polling the press in early August, *The Outlook* could find only one stanch defender of the Secretary's position—the *News and Courier* of Charleston, South Carolina. Bryan, this paper held, was entitled to a vacation, and if he preferred to use it in lecturing, that was his business. A lecturer was a teacher, and so regarded by the people; he was entitled to compensation no less than other teachers, including those who taught from the pulpit.

The vast majority condemned the Secretary roundly. Bryan's plight, the Los Angeles *Tribune* asserted, "may appeal to the sympathies of plutocrats who flick away many $12,000 bagatelles on passing whims, but hardly of the millions of real commoners who have thought differently about his social standards."

"This man is money mad," the Philadelphia *Ledger* said bitterly; "he has lost all sense of proportion; he glibly demonstrates that, in his inordinate congenital egotism, he actually believes that he is doing the American nation a signal favor by sacrificing himself and a part of his chances to tuck away each year his 'usual $10,000' of savings above his expenses, by taking charge of the affairs of state. . . . This enemy of capital, this disturber of the peace, this champion of manhood and patriotism against greed, this wordy haranguer on the sacred duty of tearing up the body politic by the roots rather than permit the 'dollar to be put above the man,' places his own dollars above his country and all mankind."

The *New York World,* a consistant Bryan supporter, offered to pay the Secretary of State $8,000 a year if he would devote full time to his official duties and refrain from lecturing for money.

The Independent took a balanced position. Are the salaries of cabinet members high enough? All knowledgeable people are aware that $12,000 a year is not enough for a Secretary of State to live on and meet his social and governmental obligations "even if . . . he substitutes at his official dinners grape juice or apollinaris for champagne."

But what do cabinet officers owe the country in return for the privilege of holding high office? To this question,

Bryan had come up with the wrong answer. The test of what he should do with his time was not what was best for his personal finances but what was best for the country. "If he can best serve the country by taking a vacation, he should take a vacation. If he can best serve the country by making a speaking tour, he should make the speaking tour. If, in times of stress and pressure, he can best serve the country by sticking at his post, regardless of vacations, or rest, or personal predilections, there he should stick."

Bryan knew, when he was invited to become Secretary of State, *The Independent* concluded, that cabinet members could not live on their salaries. If he were not willing to accept a financial sacrifice he should not have taken the office.

The Nation made the same point. "It is doubtless true that $12,000 will not cover the expenses to which the Secretary of State is put. But there stands the office and the salary; it can be accepted or declined. Once accepted, the pecuniary consequences should be accepted also without whining."

The Nation, more incisively than any other publication, expressed the widespread belief that Bryan's performances were in shockingly bad taste. An editorial entitled "The Bryan Scandal" pointed out that at Emporia, Kansas, Bryan had enjoyed the following billing:

New York City Marine Band
Avon Sketch Club
English Opera Quintet
Neopolitan Troubadours
William Jennings Bryan
Elliot A. Boyl

Sears, the Taffy Man
Lorenzo Zwickey
Ed. Amhurst Ott

"We are deeply outraged," the editorial continued, "by the spectacle of the Secretary of State appearing nightly under canvas for pay, or a part of the gate receipts, in company with acrobats and vaudeville performers of every kind. . . . We have no quarrel because the Secretary of State wishes to meet crowds of his fellow-citizens and draw inspiration from them. But we do protest emphatically at what is now going on—a Secretary of State cutting short conferences with foreign Ambassadors to rush off to a little town in West Virginia or Maryland to earn his $250; then returning to Washington by sleeper for a few hours at his office, and finally dashing off again for a wild night ride by auto or a train journey to some obscure hamlet. There, it is obvious, he appears not before a real old-fashioned Chautauqua—which was a dignified university extension type of movement—but before a vaudeville audience."

"If Mr. Bryan will take our advice," *The Nation* concluded, "he will cease defending these performances and either resign his position forthwith . . . or rest his case squarely upon his having the President's sanction for his performances."

Had Bryan chosen the second course, Mr. Dooley knew what the President's answer would have been. The philosopher of Archer Road had sensed that Wilson had no high opinion of his first minister, and was determined to be his own Secretary of State.

"Bryan?" Mr. Dooley asked. "O', he's all right. I see

be the dhramatic pa-pers that he's restin'. He's had a fine season. He knocked thim cold in Dubuque, kilt thim in Peory, an' turned thim away in Kankykee. He's goin' to change his act nex' year an' play his lecture on a piccolo while suspinded from a thrapeze. Th' British minister called on him th' other day an' discovered him practicin' a handspring. Is the prisidint sore on him? Why shud he be? On th' conthry, he likes it. Iv all William Jennings Bryan's frinds none has offered him more encouragement in his stage career thin Woodrow Wilson. 'Can ye lave Washin'ton f'r a few weeks?' says he. 'Can ye? Why, me dear frind, ye can go away an' stay a year. There's nawthin' in the state department that I can't attind to. I wish ye ivry success in the wurruld!"

The fall saw the big golf tournaments. In mid-September Francis Ouimet took the United States Open at the Country Club, Brookline, Massachusetts, with Harry Vardon and Edward Ray coming in second and third. Shortly afterward, at Garden City, Long Island, J. D. Travers defeated J. G. Anderson for the United States Amateur championship. In October, at Wilmington, Delaware, an English golfer, Miss G. Ravenscroft, defeated Miss M. Hollins of the United States for the title in the United States Women's Amateur meet.

As in the case of the Davis Cup matches, only a handful of Americans were interested.

(In my boyhood, even when I was in high school, to mention golf was to make jokes about "cow pasture pool."

It was a game played at a place on the edge of town called the country club—a place which no one in my group had ever seen except at a distance, and which we had no desire to see at close range. Golf players lived for the most part on inherited money, and their accounts at my father's store were often hard to collect. No envy, I am sure, colored our attitude. I long ago overcame my scorn for golf and golf players, but I confess that I still harbor a mild prejudice against country clubs.)

Woodrow Wilson to Mrs. Mary A. Hulbert, September 7:

"Every now and again, just to keep my hand in and feel natural, I break a precedent. I broke one today, feeling a little stale and dull. I went to church in a white linen suit. It was simply so hot that I could not stand any other kind. I created a mild sensation as I entered the church, as I could see by the way people looked at me; but that of course is what every public man wishes to do, at church or anywhere else, and it did not in the least interfere with my own state of mind during the service. After the first five minutes I lost the self-consciousness I had felt on entering. Is there anything more hateful or more unhandsome and ridiculous than self-consciousness? I would rather have the small pox."

AUTUMN

Although people might wonder how girls could live on a weekly wage of $5.00 and feel sorry for those who had to, they continued to be fascinated with opulence. Thus the "last night" ball on the new and fashionable *Imperator*, due to arrive at New York on September 21, was news even to the inland *Chicago Tribune*. At least $1,000,000,000, the reporter estimated, was represented in the ship's ballroom. Among those present were:

Elbert H. Gary and wife. Chairman of the board, United States Steel Corporation, with a personal fortune of $50,000,000.

Mr. and Mrs. Harry Payne Whitney and their daughter Flora. Whitney was understood to have inherited not less than $40,000,000 from his father.

Bernard M. Baruch, "well known on the Street as 'Barney,'" and said to have made $20,000,000 in the market.

James Cutting of New York and Newport. Reported as engaged to the "wealthy and beautiful widow," Mrs. William B. Leeds.

Louis C. Tiffany. His father's estate was estimated at $30,000,000.

Charles T. Crocker, grandson of a California '49'er, and credited with a fortune of $20,000,000.

John R. Drexel, Philadelphia banker, and Oscar Straus, New York merchant prince, both men of great wealth.

Jules S. Bache, New York banker.

Mrs. Oliver H. P. Belmont, whose husband was supposed to have left her $5,000,000.

Mrs. W. K. Vanderbilt.

The *Tribune* reported: "The affair took place in the rose ballroom, a large and beautiful apartment. . . . And here's a fashion tip from the highest circles: according to an observant eyewitness, every one of the women present wore a slit skirt. But, though they tangoed briskly, they were most discreet and modest about it. No standards of propriety were set at defiance."

Two months later newspaper coverage of the opening night of the Chicago opera season offered additional evidence of public interest in the very rich. The opera, "Tosca," attracted far less attention than the audience. The *Tribune* went to unusual lengths to describe the costumes worn by the leaders of society. Mrs. E. T. Stotesbury of Philadelphia, who had come with her husband for the performance, took first place. Along with her carmine chiffon velvet gown she wore a wide dog collar of diamonds, a rope of great stones which hung almost to her knees, a chain from which dangled pear-shaped stones of enormous size, diamond ear drops, and a tiara made of interlapping circles of diamonds. A private detective accompanied her even to the ladies' retiring room. A similar tiara, although narrower, adorned the coiffure of Mrs. W. J. Chalmers, who also wore diamond hair ornaments and diamond ear drops. Mrs. Cyrus McCormick, attired in blue pompadour satin with a bodice of rose point lace veiled in mauve chiffon, had a collar of pearls and diamonds, an emerald necklace, and a diamond tiara. Mrs. Harry Gordon Selfridge of London, formerly of Chicago, was notable for a "hair band of great pearls, surrounded by diamonds," with a necklace "from which hung drapes of diamonds heavy enough to cover almost the entire throat." A "gorgeous" rope of pearls, a dog collar, and tiara of diamonds embellished the silver and blue brocaded gown of Mrs. George M. Pullman. Mrs. Pullman's daughter, Mrs. Frank O. Lowden, was a stunning figure in brilliant red velvet, diamond tiara, and collar of pearls and diamonds.

Not to slight anyone, the *Tribune* devoted nearly two columns to the costumes of 120 other women, their names arranged in alphabetical order, and another column to a listing of the occupants of boxes.

The baseball season of 1913, coming to an end in early October, held few surprises. The Philadelphia Athletics under their fifty-one-year-old manager Connie Mack (Cornelius McGillicuddy) had taken first place in the American League on April 24. Although they were pushed at times by Cleveland and Washington they held the top position all season. Boston, pennant winner in 1912, folded early in the season and ended up in fourth place. The owners of the team shocked fans the country over by discharging, in mid-season, a manager (Garland Stahl) who had brought home a world championship only a few months earlier. The newest manager in the league, Frank Chance, former "Peerless Leader" of the Chicago Cubs, faced the fact before the season ever opened that he was saddled with mediocrities and would have to be satisfied with a place in the second division. (His Yankees held seventh place when the season closed.)

In the National League the New York Giants, under the dynamic John J. McGraw, their manager for eleven years, had played erratic ball. At one time they had dropped to eighth place but by the middle of July they had climbed to the head of the league, a spot from which they were never dislodged.

In considerable part, the Giants owed the pennant to Christy Mathewson, one of the greatest pitchers of all time. Although thirty-three years old, and coming to the end of his career, Mathewson had one of his best seasons, and the best record of all National League pitchers. He appeared in forty games, finished twenty-five, won twenty-five, struck out ninety-three batters, and enjoyed an earned run average of 2.06.

The Giants went into the World Series on October 7 as underdogs. Larry Doyle, second baseman, had been hurt in an automobile accident a few days before the series began. Fred Snodgrass, centerfielder, limped on an injured leg. Fred Merkle, first baseman, sprained his ankle in the first game. And in practice before the second game John T. Meyers, catcher, split his hand.

It was not surprising, then, that the Athletics should take the series, four games out of five. The redoubtable Mathewson won the second game for the Giants, 3 to 0, breaking a tie score in the tenth inning with a base hit, but even he was vanquished, 3 to 1, when he pitched again in the fifth and last game. The Athletics, with a pitching staff which included the Chippewa Indian, "Chief" Bender, and the Gettysburg collegian "Eddie" Plank, were simply too strong for McGraw's contenders.

Reviewing the season, John B. Foster, editor of *Spaldings Official Baseball Guide,* commented on one of the deficiencies of the Giants in the series, indeed, throughout the season: their weakness at the bat. "There are not a few who credit it to too much driving in motor cars. Some of the most expert oculists insist that athletes, who are dependent upon clearness of vision for success in physical competition, should under no circumstances become addicted to the motor car habit."

Foster had another comment which the owners of teams in the newly organized Federal League, ambitious to transform the circuit into a rival of the two major leagues, should have taken to heart:

"Notwithstanding the banner patronage enjoyed [during the year] it is safe to say that less coin of the realm remained in the coffers of the club owners than in some of the earlier years of their enterprise, after all bills had been settled. This was due to the increased cost of operating a major league club, which has more than doubled in a period of a dozen years. Practically everything connected with the promotion of the pastime has gone up in cost, and the club owners, as a whole, are getting smaller returns on their investments than formerly. Higher salaries paid the players are not the only element in this increased cost. The larger number of players now carried on the payroll raises the total cost considerably, and the transportation expense is increased."

Seven days out of Rotterdam the *SS Volturno* of the Uranium Steamship Company, 3,600 tons, approached Halifax, where she was to stop before proceeding to New York, her ultimate destination. In addition to her crew of ninety-three she carried 564 passengers, mostly emigrants from southeastern Europe. Her hold was loaded with oils and chemicals of various kinds, peat moss, wines and liquors, bales of burlap, rags, and cotton.

At 6:55 A.M. on October 9 fire was discovered in a forward hold. The flames spread fast. The ship's radio—wireless it was called then—sent out an urgent call for help. Lifeboats were lowered. All except two were smashed by the heavy seas; these sank with their occupants.

At 11.00 A.M. the *Carmania*, first of twelve rescue ships to reach the scene, made her appearance. Strong winds and mountainous waves made it impossible for their lifeboats, which they bravely launched, to take passengers from the *Volturno*. The captain of the *Carmania,* largest of the rescuers, finally placed the ship as a shield against the wind. Thus protected, lifeboats fished from the water a few bold spirits who dropped from the deck of the stricken vessel. Most of the passengers preferred to huddle on the stern.

During the night the wind abated. A tanker, the *Narragansett,* poured out oil, and the remaining passengers and crew were taken aboard the hovering ships without further loss of life. Of a total ship's company of 657, 532 were saved. The last to leave the doomed ship was her captain, Francis Inch, exhausted and almost blind from heat and smoke. "One of the bravest men I ever saw" was the comment of Edward Lloyd, the *Volturno's* second officer.

Comparisons with the fate of the *Titanic* eighteen months earlier were inevitable. In that disaster only 706 persons in a total of 2,223 had been saved. The *Titanic's* officers and crew had behaved badly; the officers and men of the *Volturno* had lived up to the finest traditions of the sea. Captain Inch had proved to be a superb seaman; so had the masters of the ships that had come to the rescue. But the great difference lay in the effectiveness of the wireless. In 1912 when the *Titanic* went down, many ships had not yet installed the device; others had day operators only. In 1913 the wireless brought a dozen ships to the scene in a few hours. Without it, all agreed, the *Volturno* would have sunk without a trace.

In the fall a bitter political battle drew the attention of the entire country to New York. In 1912 Charles F. Murphy, head of Tammany Hall, had picked William Sulzer as the Democratic candidate for governor of New York. Once elected, Sulzer, an undistinguished congressman since 1895 and hitherto a docile Tammany lieutenant, decided to be his own man. In the spring of 1913 he broke with Murphy over patronage, and then offered the boss a further affront by backing a bill to replace the state nominating conventions with a direct primary. The legislature, under Murphy's control, refused to pass the direct primary bill; Sulzer vetoed two bills retaining the convention system.

On June 16 Sulzer called a special session of the legislature to consider his own legislation. Murphy decided that the time had come to crush the upstart. A joint committee, dominated, of course, by Tammany, was appointed to investigate rumors of impropriety in Sulzer's conduct, both before and after his election. After some floundering the committee struck ore—not rich ore, but good enough for its purpose. On August 13 the investigators presented eight articles of impeachment to the lower house. The charges boiled down to four:

1. Sulzer had violated the penal statutes of New York by filing a false statement of campaign receipts and expenses, notably in not reporting eleven specific contributions aggregating $8,500. Named among the donors: Jacob H. Schiff of Kuhn, Loeb and Company, $2,500; and Henry Morgenthau, president of Henry Morgenthau Company, bankers, $1,000.
2. Sulzer had converted to his own use campaign contributions totaling $32,850, with which he had speculated in stocks.
3. He had "corruptly" used his influence as governor to affect the price of securities in which he was interested.
4. He had attempted to coerce witnesses called to testify before the joint committee.

At this stage in the proceedings—on September 2 to be exact—Theodore Roosevelt wrote to the embattled governor:

"I believe I thoroughly understand the assault that is now being made upon you. I have yet to meet a single person who believes, or even pretends to believe, that a single honest motive has animated the proceedings of your antagonists. From Mr. Murphy himself to the legislators who obeyed his direction, there is no possible question that all of your assailants are the enemies of the public, that their aim is to acquire the evil domination of the State Government, and that the conspiracy against you has not one saving impulse behind it that can in the remotest degree be ascribed to patriotism or civic spirit or to anything save the basest impulse of crooked politics."

But Roosevelt was far from sure of his man. "Let me add one thing, my dear Governor," he wrote. "You owe it to yourself and to all those who have supported you to take the earliest opportunity to answer the charges made against you. . . . I very earnestly hope that as soon as possible the explanation and answer will be made."

Sulzer's first opportunity to defend himself came on September 18 when the Court of Impeachment, consisting of the Senate and the nine judges of the Court of Appeals, convened. The governor's counsel tried to have the charges thrown out on the ground that the articles were voted while the assembly sat in special session, that a special session could consider only the subjects included in the governor's call, and that impeachment was not one of these. By a vote of fifty to one the court ruled that the impeachment was valid, and the trial proceeded.

Sulzer entered a formal denial of all the charges. Testimony and arguments took almost a month. The governor's lawyers pictured him as a harmless, well-meaning man whose difficulties stemmed from his naiveté. As one put it: "The respondent is a plain, affable man, easy to approach and a man who until 1913 never made enemies. He has never had any business education or experience. . . . While a lawyer by profession, about the only evidence of that fact, as one witness stated it, is that he had a law office. He never kept books of account or records of his transactions. He is exceedingly careless and unmethodical. Details are something to which he is almost a stranger." (One wonders what qualifications he had for office.)

The defense ridiculed the characterization. Louis A. Sarecky, Sulzer's former private secretary, testified that he had prepared the account of contributions and expenditures. Sulzer merely glanced at it and asked, "Is this all right?" "This is as accurate as I could get it," the secretary replied. Alton B. Parker, one of the prosecuting attorneys, countered that the testimony proved only that Sarecky was well trained. Sulzer, Parker said, "must indeed have chuckled at the wisdom of Sarecky when he glanced over this list, for he did not see in that list the checks of bankers like Jacob H. Schiff; there were not to be found in that list the checks of his brewery friends; not a single check could he discover there of a politician, whether leader of the organization, district leader or otherwise. Even Morgenthau, with his $1,000, did not appear. Not a single dollar was there representing any of the great interests in New York. . . . The man who read that list and examined it knew that it was not true. It does not help him for the boy to say he did the best he could. His master, William Sulzer, knew it was a lie."

On October 17 the Court of Impeachment found Sulzer guilty of perjury in connection with his declaration of campaign contributions and expenses and guilty of using threats to suppress testimony before the investigating committee. The next day he was removed from office. He became the seventh governor in the history of the United States to be impeached, the third to be convicted and removed from office.

Many contemporaries, blind to Sulzer's ethical frailties, pictured him as a hero, the victim of Tammany's evil vengeance. Running as an independent, he was elected, on November 3, to the New York Assembly polling twice as many votes as his opponents combined.

"Bryan is, I really believe, the most contemptible figure we have ever had as Secretary of State."

The judgment, expressed in a letter which Theodore Roosevelt wrote to Senator Henry Cabot Lodge on September 9, was harsh enough, but one wonders what it might have been a month later. For on October 9, in *The Independent,* Bryan presented his views on arbitration at some length. This was the policy, already inaugurated in the first weeks of the administration, which he hoped would win him a place in history. It was also the policy which infuriated the belligerent former President, to whom national interest and national honor were not subject to adjudication.

"War," Bryan began, "is a matter of feeling rather than a matter of logic. It cannot settle anything that could not be better settled in a better way. There is no more reason why nations should fight out their differences on the battlefield than why individuals should settle their differences by physical force. . . . As nations differ greatly in size and strength, it is obvious that war cannot be relied upon to establish justice any more than a fight between two individuals can be relied upon to determine which is in the right."

The Secretary of State rehashed old arguments. Wicked and selfish men—the makers and purveyors of armor plate and battleships and munitions—favored war, but the people, exercising more and more control over their governments, were coming to recognize that they were the ones who paid the price in taxes and blood. This the rulers saw clearly. Problems, national and international, had multiplied to such an extent that at no other time in history had there been so many differences that could lead to war. Yet at no other time in history had the world been more at peace with itself.

Bryan also reviewed the arbitration treaties which, with Wilson's approval, he had proposed to foreign envoys in April. The distinctive feature of his proposal, as he saw it, was the fact that for the first time in international agreements of this kind no subject could be withheld from arbitration. Twenty-six nations, he reported, had already "favorably considered" the proposals.

"Taken altogether," the Secretary of State concluded, "conditions promising world peace and prosperity were never more favorable than now, and in saying this I have special reference to those wars that might occur between great powers, which sooner or later would involve other powers—wars that would cost hundreds of millions in money, the lives of hundreds and thousands of men, and in time would consume months and perhaps years."

Apparently the American Secretary of State saw no significance in the fact that six months before his article appeared Germany had increased her appropriation for military preparation by $500,000,000 a year, while France had begun calling up conscripts for three years instead of two.

To Roosevelt, Wilson was at least as deplorable a national misfortune as Bryan. "I regard Wilson with contemptuous dislike," Roosevelt had written to Lodge. "He has ability of a certain kind, and he has the nerve that his type so often shows in civil and domestic affairs where there is no danger of physical violence. He will jump up and down on cheap politicians, and bully and cajole men in public life who are anxious not to part company with their political chief. But he is a ridiculous creature in international matters. He is a narrow and bitter partisan, and he is intellectually thoroughly dishonest."

A few weeks later, at a Progressive Party dinner in New York, Roosevelt publicly attacked the President, although not by name. He reminded his audience that during his first administration Santo Domingo was shaken by a series of revolutions until near-anarchy prevailed and the lives and property of Americans living there were jeopardized. "I never said I would refuse to run the risk of shedding a drop of blood to protect American property. Nor did I say that all American citizens should leave the country, abandoning their property to the good will of the contending factions."

The former President emphasized again the chasm that separated Wilson's Mexican policy from his own concept of foreign relations: "Nor did I refuse to act at all until foreign powers acted, nor either ask or accept their cooperation in action; still less did I follow a course which was certain to produce anarchy and make existing conditions worse so as to force intervention."

Roosevelt reserved the full expression of his animosity toward Wilson for a long article on the Progressive Party which he published in *The Century* for October. Nothing could be hoped for from the Republicans—a party which had given "absolute control of its destinies into the hands of a National Committee composed of fifty-three irresponsible and on the whole obscure politicians." After six months in office the Democrats had displayed "discreditable impotence in foreign affairs," while in domestic legislation their only achievement was a tariff that was no more than "a red herring dragged across the trail to divert our people from the real issues."

Democratic promises, moveover, held out no hope for curing the nation's economic ills. At this point Roosevelt mixed personal animus with partisanship. He wrote:

"I have read with care Mr. Wilson's chapter in *The New Freedom* in which he professes to set forth his attitude as regards the trusts. The chapter does not contain, as far as I can find, one specific proposal for affirmative action. It does contain repeated, detailed, and specific misrepresentations of the Progressive position—misrepresentations so gross that all that is necessary in order to refute them is to challenge Mr. Wilson to produce a single line from the Progressive National platform, or from the speeches of the men who stood on that platform, which will bear out his assertions. Aside from these specific misrepresentations, there are various well-phrased general statements implying approval of morality in the abstract, but no concrete proposal for affirmative action. A patient and sincere effort to find out what Mr. Wilson means by the New Freedom leaves me in some doubt whether it has any meaning at all. But if there is any meaning, the phrase means and can mean only freedom for the big man to prey unchecked on the little man, freedom for unscrupulous exploiters of the public and of labor to continue unchecked in a career of cutthroat commercialism, wringing their profits out of the laborers whom they oppress and the business rivals and the public whom they outwit. This is the only possible meaning that the phrase can have if reduced to action. It is, however, not probable that it has any meaning at all. It certainly can have no meaning of practical value if its coiner will not translate it out of the realm of magniloquent rhetoric into specific propositions affecting the intimate concerns of our social and industrial life to-day."

A reviewer who attacks a book immoderately may expect to find the same treatment accorded to his own work. Most reviewers praised *Theodore Roosevelt: An Autobiography* when it came out in the fall of 1913, but *The Nation* paid back the author for what he had written about *The New Freedom.* In the *Autobiography, The Nation's* reviewer wrote, "there is almost no raising of the curtain, no revelation of that 'inside history' which makes memoirs at once so fascinating and so valuable." A "terrible earnestness" featured the book, and the reader would look in vain for any evidence of a sense of humor. The author took up his deeds one by one, recounted them briefly, and then "immersed them in a flood of explanation and justification." Only one chapter, "Outdoors and Indoors," deserved real praise.

Two succeeding generations have been more charitable.

On September 9, in a rare moment of candid confession, the President wrote to Mrs. Wilson, whose delicate health had dictated a summer's residence at Cornish, New Hampshire: "Mexico is *sui generis.* I do not know what to make of it. The apparent situation changes like quicksilver. But the real situation, I fancy, remains the same, and is likely to yield to absent treatment."

In truth, since the inauguration of the "watchful waiting" policy, relations between Mexico and the United States had seemed to be less brittle. Huerta had scheduled a presidential election for October 26 and had promised that it would be fairly conducted. Wilson had indicated that the United States would recognize, as the lawful head of the Mexican state, whomever the voters chose. But neither Wilson nor Bryan could see that they were living in an unreal world. They were ignoring the fact that Carranza's Constitutionalists controlled far more of the country than Huerta's forces, and that the Constitutionalists represented the only hope of satisfying the poverty-stricken and landless masses. When William Bayard Hale returned to Washington in late September he broke Wilson's complacency by reminding him that the United States had made no genuine approach to Carranza, and by asserting emphatically that no settlement which ignored him could last.

Bryan, as disturbed as his chief, immediately sounded out Carranza. Would the leader of the Constitutionalists join in an armistice and agree to a general election? By October 7 the Secretary of State had his answer: Carranza would not stand for an election in which his enemies controlled the machinery of voting. He had no intention of agreeing to a partition of the country: he intended to conquer it *in toto.*

On October 8 the city of Torreón, key to Huerta's defenses in northern Mexico, fell to Carranza's forces. Two days later the Chamber of Deputies, center of opposition to Huerta's regime even though it sat under the provisional president's menacing frown, threatened to move the capital to a point within the Constitutionalist lines. Huerta threw troops around the Chamber, arrested 110 deputies, and assumed full dictatorial powers until a new Chamber should be elected, presumably on October 26. Soon afterward he announced that he was not a candidate for the presidency and would not accept the office if elected.

Wilson fumed. In anger and frustration he composed a note to Nelson O'Shaughnessy, U.S. Chargé d'Affaires at Mexico City, denouncing Huerta's "lawless methods" and asserting that his dissolution of the Congress had destroyed "all possibility of a free and fair election." No matter what the result, the United States would not accept it.

With Bryan, the President set out to forestall European recognition of any Mexican government that might be chosen in the promised election. Notes to be sent to the American Embassy at Mexico City and the Powers represented there were prepared. But John Bassett Moore, Counselor of the State Department, persuaded his superior and the President that the circular to the Powers would do more harm than good. Wilson was mollified, temporarily, by assurances from London that Great Britain, suspected by the Americans of supporting Huerta behind the scences, would follow the lead of the United States in whatever measures she might take.

The long-awaited election took place as scheduled. When the results were in the congress declared that none of the three candidates—Gamboa, Félix Díaz, and Calero

—had been elected. The delegates proceeded to designate Huerta president ad interim until July, 1914, when new elections would be held.

Wilson decided to discard "watchful waiting" and to take personal charge of a campaign to get rid of Huerta. The President's first move: new instructions (November 1) to O'Shaughnessy in Mexico City, which were to be shown to all the foreign representatives stationed there.

Unless Huerta "voluntarily and as if of his own motion" retired from authority, Wilson warned, he would issue an ultimatum requiring the dictator's abdication. If rejected, the President of the United States would propose "very serious practical measures"—meaning active aid to the Constitutionalists—to Congress. To fill the void at Mexico City he urged that some man or small group of men enjoying public confidence be constituted a provisional government, and that general elections be held at an early date. The note concluded: "That some such course, approved by the Government of the United States, is now absolutely necessary, that government being firmly and irrevocably resolved, by one method or another, to cut the government of Huerta off, if he persists, from all outside aid or countenance, and Huerta will only for a very few days longer be free to act with apparent freedom of choice in the matter. His retirement and an absolutely free field for a constitutional rehabilitation being the least the United States can accept. This Government cannot too earnestly urge him to make the inevitable choice wisely and in full view of the terrible consequences of hesitation or refusal."

On November 3 O'Shaughnessy presented Wilson's ultimatum, for that it was, to Huerta's secretary. At first the dictator seemed disposed to give in, but in a few days he decided on defiance. On November 8 he dispatched a circular note to the foreign envoys affirming the constitutionality of his regime and avowing his determination to remain in power until he had pacified all Mexico. On the same day Wilson attacked again, also with a circular note to the Powers. "While the President does not feel that he can yet announce his policy with regard to Mexico in detail," he stated, "he feels he should make known . . . in advance his clear judgment that it is his immediate duty to require Huerta's retirement from the Mexican government and that this government must now proceed to employ such means as may be necessary to secure this result."

Next, the President belatedly attempted to come to an understanding with the Constitutionalists. Again he called on his old friend, William Bayard Hale. Hale was to find out whether Carranza would accept the co-operation of the United States in setting up a constitutional regime in Mexico City. "Co-operation" meant lifting the arms embargo. But Carranza, far more antiforeign than Huerta, must be told plainly that he would have to respect the lives and property of foreigners.

Between November 12 and 18 Hale met several times with Carranza and his cabinet. In the end the American emissary had to admit failure. Carranza wanted arms and ammunition eagerly enough, but he would agree to no conditions in order to obtain them. "The Constitutionalists," he declared formally, "refused to admit the right of any nation on this continent acting alone or in conjunction with European Powers to interfere in the domestic affairs of the Mexican Republic; that they held the idea of armed intervention from outside as unconceivable and inadmissible upon any grounds or upon any pretext."

Wilson had come to a dead end. Huerta would not behave as a decent man should. Carranza would not cooperate. And the American people, Wilson well knew, would not support armed intervention. But he could always write another note. This one, dated November 24, took the form of a circular to the foreign envoys:

"Usurpations like that of General Huerta menace the peace and development of America as nothing else could. They not only render the development of ordered self-government impossible; they also tend to set law entirely aside, to put the lives and fortunes of citizens and foreigners alike in constant jeopardy, to invalidate contracts and concessions in any way the usurper may devise for his own profit, and to impair both the national credit and all the foundations of business, domestic or foreign.

"It is the purpose of the United States, therefore, to discredit and defeat such usurpations whenever they occur. The present policy of the Government of the United States is to isolate General Huerta entirely; to cut him off from foreign sympathy and aid and from domestic credit, whether moral or material, and so to force him out.

"It hopes and believes that isolation will accomplish this end, and shall await the results without irritation or impatience. If General Huerta does not retire by force of circumstances, it will become the duty of the United States to use less peaceful means to put him out."

With this blast the President reverted to "watchful waiting." W. Morgan Shuster, lawyer, publisher, and publicist, writing in *The Century Magazine* summed up the Mexican situation as it stood at the end of the year.

"One Victoriano Huerta, styling himself President of Mexico, and a hundred times hailed in official bulletins at Washington as the pirate king 'about to go,' is still at the head of the Mexican Government and army, and in complete control of the capital and some outlying states and cities. He sits in his castle, a grim, apparently unshaken old usurper; he leers at his minister of foreign affairs, receives with all formality the accredited ministers of most other nations of the world, sends his dispatches to his envoys at the capitals of Europe, warmly embraces the American Chargé d'Affaires at a public reception, and sends his compliments to the 'great American people'; but the world is asked to believe that he must go. The moral edict has gone forth. Huerta himself doubtless knows that he cannot last forever. Whether it will be by the victory of the wine-cellar, by the hands of an assassin, by the shell or bullet of a besieging rebel army, or from so-called natural causes, it is of course true that sooner or later Huerta must go. Meanwhile, however, he continues to make sport of the situation, and if he himself is not enjoying it, certainly no one else is."[1]

---

[1] *In 1914 relations with Mexico grew worse steadily. On April 24, as a climax to a silly dispute about saluting the American flag, Wilson ordered Admiral Frank F. Fletcher, commanding a naval force off Veracruz, to take the city. Wilson had not expected bloodshed, but Mexican naval cadets and civilians resisted, with the result that the American forces suffered about ninety casualties, the Mexicans 300. Three days later both Mexico and the United States agreed to submit the question to arbitration by Argentina, Brazil, and Chile. Continued control of the Veracruz customhouse by the United States cut off Huerta's revenues and forced him to resign and leave the country. On August 20, 1914, the Constitutionalists occupied Mexico City.*

But the Carranza forces soon fell to fighting among themselves. Civil war continued. Wilson, absorbed in problems posed by war in Europe,

In the midst of the Mexican imbroglio, the Senate struggled with the Federal Reserve Act, or the Currency Bill, as it was more often called.

On June 26, Carter Glass had introduced the measure in the House. There the Democrats had a safe majority, but many of the party radicals were far from satisfied. Wilson gave Glass every ounce of support he could, inviting doubtful Congressmen to the White House and subjecting them to his very considerable powers of persuasion. When Glass, temper frayed by snipers within his own ranks, threatened to resign, Wilson burst out with one of his rare expletives: "Damn it, don't resign, old fellow; outvote them!"

The discussion, often acrimonious, lasted more than a week. Bryan brought it to an end by a letter to Glass: "You are authorized," the Secretary wrote, "to speak for me and say that I appreciate so profoundly the service rendered by the President to the people in the stand he has taken on the fundamental principles involved in currency reform, that I am with him in all the details. If

---

paid little attention to the unhappy nation until the spring of 1916, when Villa, now a bitter enemy of Carranza, his former chief, shot up Columbus, New Mexico, killing many of the inhabitants. With Carranza's consent, Wilson sent a cavalry expedition under General John J. Pershing into Mexico to find and punish Villa. The expedition never caught up with the Mexican leader. After nearly a year, the troops were quietly withdrawn. In a month or two the United States declared war on Germany. Americans forgot about Mexico. Many Mexicans remembered, and for a long time.

my opinion has influence with anyone called upon to act on this measure, I am willing to assume full responsibility for what I do when I advise him to stand by the President and assist in securing the passage of the bill at the earliest possible moment."

The opposition fell apart, and the caucus made the bill a party measure by an overwhelming vote. But the opposition continued. "Capital must be managed by those who supply it," asserted George M. Reynolds, president of the Continental and Commercial National Bank of Chicago, "and the investor must be free to decide whether or not he shall make investments." The editor of the *Texas Banker Record* described the bill as a "communistic idea that is sought to be written into the financial statutes of the country. If such a bill passes," he continued, "history will write President Wilson as a complete failure and Bryan will once more have ruined the chances of the Democratic party." Many other bankers and editors spoke in the same vein. Yet the House, unintimidated, passed the bill by a vote of 287 to 85 on September 18.

Like the tariff, the bill faced much rougher weather in the Senate. There the Democratic margin was much narrower, the conservative influence more potent, the lobby more effective. The opposition sought delay by every means at its command, hoping to wear out a Congress tired from the labors and heat of a Washington summer.

The Senators wanted to go home. Wilson refused to give them any respite. Delay, he believed, would signify weakness. On September 10 he called the Democratic Steering Committee of the Senate to the White House and informed its members that he was opposed to any adjournment of more than three days' duration. He also declared that he would resist strenuously any material amendments. "You may be sure," he wrote, "that there will be no budging here with regard to the essential features of the currency bill."

The bankers continued to fight. The American Bankers' Association condemned the bill; so did the United States Chamber of Commerce. Most members of the financial community were incapable, because of experience and habit, of considering the proposed legislation on its merits. They feared any change in a system, no matter how imperfect, which they knew well and could command completely. "Hurley, the bankers don't know what they want," Wilson exploded in a letter to the president of the First National Bank of Wheaton, Illinois. "They are too much in the atmosphere of the thing. They do not see it as a whole, nor do they look into the future."

By mid-October, the currency bill was stalled. Many members of Congress were willing to drop the whole business. Wall Street was nervous, the nation confused. The President showed signs of strain. A visitor was "shocked to see him look so worn. The change since January last is terribly marked, and you [Edward M. House] ought to try and force him to take a week's complete rest the moment the strain is relaxed—even at the sacrifice of some public business."

Wilson himself confessed his fatigue to a friend, Mrs. Mary A. Hulbert. "I have been under a terrible strain, if the truth must be told," he wrote, "and am still under it, and my little spell of indigestion (for that is what it was) was due, undoubtedly, to my being worn out and unable to run both my stomach and the government. I realize when I stop to think about it all that I never before knew such a strain as I have undergone ever since Congress convened in April. The more I succeed in directing things the more I am depended on for leadership and expected to do everything, make all paths straight and carry every plan to its completion. . . . I was a bit bored this past week to find myself so 'poorly' that I almost lost interest in golf itself and lay down to rest instead of going out to play. . . . But that is all gone by now. For one thing the weather has changed. The lassitude that was in the air has been replaced . . . by bracing airs, and I am feeling very different—all my spunk came back!"

The tide turned soon. Wilson, Bryan, McAdoo, and House worked on the most influential Senators in revolt: Reed of Missouri, O'Gorman of New York, Hitchcock of Nebraska. On October 20 O'Gorman capitulated by giving the *New York World* an interview favoring the bill. Reed also surrendered. Wilson wrote to the Missouri Senator: "I want to thank you very warmly and sincerely for your statement made through a New York newspaper. I have felt all along the sincere honesty and independence of judgment you are exercising in this whole matter, and you may be sure that there has never been in my mind any criticism except an occasional difference of judgment."

Hitchcock remained on the fence, but with O'Gorman and Reed in the fold, the President could do without him. On October 20 Wilson informed Underwood, who had told him that members of the House were restive at being held in Washington and wanted to know when they might expect to be released: "I feel confident that a report on the bill may be expected not later than the first week in November. . . . I believe that the action of the Senate upon the bill will follow within two or, at the most, three weeks after the report is made. . . . Senators on both sides realize that the business of the country awaits this legislation, impatient of being kept in suspense, and display a most public spirited desire to dispose of it promptly. The passage of the bill is assured."

Still, the bankers would not give up. Through Frank A. Vanderlip, president of the National City Bank of New York, an eastern group attempted to substitute an entirely new measure for the Glass-Owen bill. Wilson refused even to see Vanderlip and the two associates, representing J. P. Morgan and Company and the Bankers' Trust Company, who had come to Washington with him. The bill before the Senate, the President said, was perfectly suited to the needs of the country. He would accept neither a substitute nor an amendment. Vanderlip and his friends returned to New York, defeated.

Democratic leaders now took the unusual step of caucusing on the Currency Bill. Hitchcock and several other dissidents announced that they would not be bound by any action in caucus, and the attempt was abandoned. The caucus did decide that there would be no adjournment for Christmas unless the bill could be passed by December 24. "A striking illustration of the discipline the President has instilled into the party ranks," the *New York Times* commented.

Late in November the banking and currency committee presented the bill to the Senate without a recommendation. On the 24th Senator Owen opened a debate which lasted three weeks.

The Republican opposition came to a climax with a speech by Elihu Root, of New York, who saw unlimited inflation and ultimate national ruin if the bill were to become law. "Ah, Mr. President," he said sadly, "we are turning our faces away from the fundamental principle upon which we have come to our high estate. We are turning them weakly toward practices which history shows have invariably led to decadence, to degradation, and the downfall of nations. We are setting our steps now in the pathway which through the protection of a paternal government brought the mighty power of Rome to its fall; and we are doing it here without a mandate from the people of the United States."

To no avail. On December 19, when the roll was called, three Republicans and one Progressive joined with fifty Democrats, all who were present, to pass the measure by a vote of 54 to 34. Differences between the House and Senate bills were speedily resolved. The bill, in final form, went to the President on December 23.

That night, surrounded by his family, members of the Cabinet, Democratic leaders of both houses, and newspapermen, he signed the Federal Reserve Act, using four pens in the process. One he handed to Glass, another to Owen, the third to McAdoo, and the fourth to Senator Chilton of West Virginia, who had provided it for the purpose. In a short informal talk after the signing the President said:

"I feel that I have had a part in completing a work which I think will be of lasting benefit to the business of the country."

Arthur Link, writing nearly fifty years later, could be far less restrained: "Thus ended the long struggle for the greatest single piece of constructive legislation of the Wilson era and one of the most important domestic Acts in this nation's history."

On November 13 the National Institute of Arts and Letters and its exalted inner circle, the American Academy of Arts and Letters, held their first meeting in Chicago. (The National Institute consisted of 250 persons eminent in art, music, or literature; the Academy was made up of fifty persons chosen by the National Institute from its own membership.)

The meeting began with a dinner at the Art Institute. Hobart C. Chatfield-Taylor, Chicago author and member of the National Institute, delivered an address of welcome; Corporation Counsel William H. Sexton, representing Mayor Harrison, also greeted the visitors. Charles L. Hutchinson, president of the Art Institute, acted as toastmaster.

Mr. Hutchinson read a letter from William Dean Howells, president of the Academy, apologizing for his inability to be present, extending greetings to his colleagues, and predicting great cultural advances for Chicago. "Chicago," he wrote, "is very near every heart that loves great and generous things, and believes them more and more possible as time goes on, and the perplexed and anxious present becomes the secure and radiant future, when all the poems and novels, the pictures and statues shall be as good as those we should each like to create. When I tell over to myself the names of the Chicagoans who have done fine and beautiful things already in those kinds I begin to envy the inspiration you will find among them."

In responding to the opening addresses William M. Sloane, chancellor of the Academy and a Columbia professor, was clearly on the defensive. Neither the National Institute nor the Academy was "a self-formed body of conceited and self-satisfied gentlemen whose purpose is to receive adulation and praise from those who do not belong." The Institute and the Academy were American in origin and aspiration. They did not consider themselves "immortals," as members of the French Academy were designated. They sought only to uphold ideals of the highest type in art and belles-lettres. Hamlin Garland clarified further the nature and purpose of the two organizations. Membership could not be bought in either, nor could social status win admission. "It is only necessary," he stated, "that a man have skill, creative power, and a fine sense of the artistic values to become a member of either institution"—a statement which left unanswered the question of the right by which these 250 persons, and they alone, judged the qualifications of all other artists and writers.

On the second day of their session, after a dinner at the Chicago Club, the "immortals," as the newspapers persisted in calling them despite their disclaimers, admitted seven new members: Brand Whitlock, author, former mayor of Toledo, Minister to Belgium; Frank Jewett Mather, Princeton professor and art critic; Francis Barton Gummere, poet and Swarthmore professor; Ashley Horace Thorndike, editor of the Tudor Shakespeare and professor of English at Columbia; Henry Bacon, designer of the Lincoln Memorial; Arthur Williams Bruner, designer of Cleveland's public square system; and Ernest Schelling, Chicago concert pianist. The Institute also bestowed its gold medal on Augustus Thomas, dramatist, for sustained excellence in his medium.

In various other sessions the members discussed a number of controversial subjects. Madison Cawein, Meredith Nicholson, and several others denounced the overemphasis on sex in contemporary literature, drama especially, but Cawein prophesied that the trend would soon change for the better. Reginald De Koven, composer, argued for opera in English. William Gillette, actor and playwright, explained the facts of life in the theater. There were only two kinds of managers, commercial and crazy, he told the idealists, and reminded them that a producer, like any other businessman, had to pay rent and meet a payroll. All other persons, even the Secretary of State, could go after money with impunity, but a theatrical manager who wanted to keep out of bankruptcy was considered the most despicable, wretchedly commercial bandit in the world.

One subject of discussion, the question of admitting women to either the Institute or the Academy, kicked up a fuss beyond the limits of Chicago. The Academy had no women as members, the Institute only one (Julia Ward Howe), and those in control made it plain that they were not about to change their policy. Brander Matthews, critic and professor of literature at Columbia, made that fact abundantly plain. "The selection of members to the Academy," he said, "is based upon universal recognition of superior accomplishment in a certain line of artistic or literary endeavor. Thus far, it appears, there are no American women who can successfully boast of such prestige."

"Amazing," said Gutzon Borglum in New York. "For the life of me I can't see how one is to divide or limit esthetics to a masculine art and a feminine art." Winthrop Ames, theatrical producer, pointed out that the French Academy had admitted Sarah Bernhardt, and that there were women on the American stage who were worthy of the highest recognition. William M. Chase, whose reputation as a painter was second to none, held that the question was not whether one was a man or a woman, but whether one was a painter. Speaking for sculptors, Daniel Chester French agreed.

And so, having spent three of their "mortal days" in Chicago, as the *Tribune* put it with barely discernible irony, and having made themselves slightly ridiculous, the "immortals" departed for their domestic eminences.

The editor of the *World Almanac* closed his section on lynchings for the year with November 12. By that date forty-five persons, all Negroes, all males, had been lynched. Three lynchings had taken place in the North—two in Illinois, one in Montana—the other forty-two in twelve states of the South and Southwest. Mississippi led with nine, Georgia and Texas came next with seven each. Thirty of the victims were accused of murder or murderous assaults; rape, alleged rape, or attempted rape accounted for nearly all the others.

In the same span of time there were eighty-one legal executions in the country.

As the *World Almanac* editor was putting these statistics together the Reverend James Owen Hannay, an Irish churchman and author, was observing the relationship between Negroes and whites in the South. In the course of a tour of the eastern United States, Hannay spent considerable time in Memphis, Tennessee. What he saw there he described in *Connaught to Chicago,* published under the pseudonym of George A. Birmingham.

"According to the theory of the American constitution the negro is a free man, a brother, as responsible as anyone else for the due ordering of the state. In actual practice the negro is either slowly emerging from the slave status or slowly sinking back to it again. It does not matter which way you look at it, the essential thing is, whichever way he is going, he is not yet settled down in either position. It is impossible—on account of the law—to treat him as a slave. It is impossible—on account of his nature, so I am told—to treat him as a free man. He is somewhere in between the two. He is economically difficult and socially undesirable."

Yet the Negro was indispensable. Even American ingenuity had not yet invented a mechanical cotton picker, and in the absence of such a machine, cotton had to be harvested by hand. The Negro supplied the hand, but not, Hannay was told, to the satisfaction of his white employers. "It is hard to get him to work at all," the Irishman wrote, "and still harder to keep him at it. . . . If he can earn enough in one day to keep him for three days he sees no sense in working during the other two."

The social position of the Negro, Hannay observed, was that of an inferior being, and the white people of the South had no intention of bettering it. "The 'man and brother' theory has broken down hopelessly, and the line drawn between the white and coloured parts of the population in the south is as well defined and distinct as any line can be. The stranger is told horrible tales of negro doings, and is convinced that the white men believe them by the precautions they take for the protection of women

There may be a good deal of exaggeration about these stories, and in any case the morality or immorality of the negro is not the most difficult element in the problem. Education, the steady enforcement of law, and the gradual pressure of civilization will no doubt in time render outrages rarer."

Hannay concluded that in the United States close contact with Negroes almost always led to a "strong, contemptuous dislike" on the part of the whites. (Had he talked with honest Negroes, he would doubtless have found that the feeling was reciprocal.) The southern American's "contempt" for the Negro was deeper than that which most people feel for those who are plainly their inferiors. "A brave man has a thoroughly intelligible contempt for one who has shown himself to be a coward. But this is an entirely different thing, different in kind, not merely in degree, from a southern white man's contempt for a negro. It is the existence of this feeling, intensely strong and very difficult to explain, which makes the problem of the negro's social future seem hopeless of solution. No moral or intellectual advance which the negro can make affects this feeling in the slightest. It is not the brutalised negro or the ignorant negro, but the negro, whom the white man refuses to recognise as a possible equal."

By November, when Hannay wrote, it had become clear that even in the government service, where Negroes had fared better than in private employment, their status had worsened. In 1912 many Negroes, traditionally Republican, had voted for Wilson in the hope that they would be included in the New Freedom. Soon after the administration took office, department heads, particularly in the Post Office and Treasury, quietly began to introduce segregation in offices, shops, rest rooms, and lunch rooms. One observer reported in late September: "No policy has been adopted in any formal sense; no Cabinet officer has issued any instructions. . . . Much of what has been done has been on the initiative of subordinate chiefs who would like to have done it long ago but dared not, or who, mostly newly-appointed Southerners, took the first opportunity."

The facts were too notorious to be denied. Criticism—from social workers, church groups, and Progressives as well as from Negro organizations—mounted as the year advanced. Even Wilson's most loyal supporter among editors, Frank Cobb of the *New York World,* condemned the new policy and placed responsibility for it upon his friend in the White House. Wilson, stung by criticism and surprised by the bitterness of the controversy, justified what had been done. "It is true," he wrote to Oswald Garrison Villard, editor of *The Nation,* "that the segregation of the colored employees in the several departments was begun upon the initiative and at the suggestion of several heads of departments, but as much in the interest of the negroes as for any other reason, with the approval of some of the most influential negroes I know, and with the idea that the friction, or rather the discontent and uneasiness, which has prevailed in many of the departments would thereby be removed. It is as far as possible from being a movement *against* the negroes. I sincerely believe it to be in their interest." When pressed for his own opinion by the editor of the *Congregationalist and Christian World* Wilson answered: "I do approve of the segregation that is being attempted in several of the departments. I have not always approved of the way the thing was done and have tried to change that in some instances for the better, but I think if you were here on the ground you would see, as I seem to see, that it is distinctly to the advantage of the colored people themselves."[1]

While beset by problems and pressures, the President and his family planned for a wedding. Early in July the engagement of Jessie Woodrow Wilson and Francis Bowes Sayre had been announced. The future bride was the second daughter, a young woman of beauty and dignity; the prospective bridegroom a twenty-eight-year-old lawyer and an assistant district attorney of New York County, New York.

When the date of the wedding—November 25—was announced the White House let it be known that the guest list would be held to a minimum. Only relatives, friends, the diplomatic corps, and the highest officials of the government would be invited. For the second time in a year this Presbyterian President who really believed in simplicity put a damper on a public festival. Democratic wheelhorses felt that their omission would be a revelation to the folks back home of their insignificance in Washing-

[1] *Arthur S. Link comments: "Although the forthright protest of the liberal North had considerable effect—the movement toward segregation in all departments was not only checked but was in part reversed in the Treasury Department—the tension between the President and the reformers on the race issue remained a source of friction for years afterward."*

ton; their wives threw small town dressmakers into despair by hastily canceling orders for gowns. Some wives of Senators nursed their resentment in silence; others moved heaven and earth to obtain invitations. Washington society was completely baffled. As one reporter in the Capital put it: "Bubbling over with good will toward the White House occupants and loving a function of this sort as a child loves a Christmas tree—the cave dwelling Washingtonians simply do not know what to make of their exclusion from the Executive Mansion."

But the President and Mrs. Wilson held to their resolution. When the Marine Band struck up the bridal chorus from "Lohengrin" at 4:30 P.M. on November 25 about 300 guests were assembled in the East Room. Members of the Cabinet, justices of the Supreme Court, foreign representatives resplendent with sashes and decorations, high government officials, a few leaders of the House and Senate (but only a few), relatives and friends watched the bridegroom, accompanied by his best man, Dr. Wilfred T. Grenfell, the "Saint of Labrador," walk up the aisle to the altar. The bridal party, the bridesmaids gowned in pale pink, preceded the President and his daughter down the main staircase. At the altar they met the groom and the two ministers who were to perform the ceremony: the Rev. Dr. Sylvester W. Beach, Presbyterian, of Princeton, and the Rev. Dr. John Nevin Sayre, Episcopalian, brother of the groom. Doctor Beach read the service, including the word "obey" at the special request of the bride. Her response emphasized her deference to tradition: to the simple avowal called for she added the words, "to be thy loving, faithful, and obedient wife." After the couple exchanged rings the procession moved to the Blue Room to the strains of Mendelssohn's "Wedding March." The reception followed.

After the reception, refreshments were served in the state dining room where the bride cut the wedding cake with the sword of Surgeon Cary T. Grayson, her father's physician and companion. No wines were served and the punch was made of fruit juice only. While the band played music for dancing the bride and groom slipped through a good-natured crowd of 5,000 people in front of the White House for a trip to Europe and then residence in Williamstown, Massachusetts, where Sayre would take a new position as assistant to the president of Williams College.

The public—or at least the female half of it—showed a lively interest in the gowns worn at the wedding. One correspondent wrote: "There were all the special features of this year's styles . . . tight draped skirts, many of them with the popular slit. Fur trimmings were almost universal. . . . Velvet, both brocaded and plain, seemed to be the most popular fabric. . . . There were coat suits and also gowns. Next to the combinations of black and white, which this year are exceptionally fascinating, came the various tones of blue. Bewildering and 'Frenchy' were the combined pink and blue frocks, a number of which were worn by younger women."

Of equal interest were the gifts showered on the young couple. In spite of the fact that from the beginning the President and Mrs. Wilson had emphasized the personal character of the wedding, many gifts came from organizations and official bodies. The House of Representatives sent a diamond chain and lavaliere, the Senate a silver tea set. From the Supreme Court came a bowl-shaped silver centerpiece. The congressional delegation from New Jersey gave two antique Persian rugs. The mountain women of Kentucky and Tennessee made enough rugs and bedspreads for a lifetime. And budding poets from all over the country showered the bride with their compositions.

It was all a kind of unofficial national holiday, but to the Wilsons the wedding had a different aspect. Of Jessie, the President wrote to a friend: "I need not tell you what effect it has had on our spirits to part with her. But Ellen has acted with noble unselfishness in hiding her distress, and I have tried to emulate her example. She lives in the house from which the dear one has now gone for good and all, while I am in the office the greater part of the time and busy with a thousand things from which I *cannot* draw my attention. My very burdens are at such juncture my blessings."

WINTER

The closing round

December approached, when the President would deliver his first annual message to Congress. A week before the event *The Independent* published an appraisal that revealed far more of the man than he would show of himself. Francis E. Leupp, the author, had begun his newspaper career in 1874 as assistant editor of the *New York Evening Post*; he had held responsible government positions, he had written biographies of Roosevelt and Taft. By experience, he was ideally equipped to place Woodrow Wilson in the recent succession of Presidents.

Many of Wilson's friends, Leupp began, feared that the new President, having spent most of his life as an educator, would try to inaugurate a nonpartisan, impersonal administration when vigorous party leadership was called for. After nine months they must have been reassured. The roster of federal appointments made after March 4 should have convinced all except the most obtuse that Wilson knew the rules. "More than one aspiring Democrat," Leupp wrote, "has turned up in Washington with a recital of his services at his tongue's end, only to be confronted with a memorandum of things he had done at home which, however well they may have pleased the party magnates there, were distinctly anti-Wilson; and that meant the end of hope for him."

Nevertheless, Wilson's academic background had colored his manners and methods. Leupp compared him with several of his predecessors. Grover Cleveland had treated the Presidency as if it were a benevolent dictatorship and had occasionally scolded Congress for not doing his bidding. Benjamin Harrison had acted as if he were his party's lawyer. McKinley listened to everyone, seemed to agree, and then did what he believed most people wanted. When Roosevelt found himself in a labyrinth he guessed the location of the exit, "then seized an ax and hewed a path to it, regardless of how the slashings fell or whom they hit." Taft weighed the pros and cons "with the serene complacency of a judge," decided questions according to the evidence—and often changed his mind overnight.

Wilson started his administration by being didactic and doctrinnaire. "His unofficial veto on the customary inaugural ball and his refusal to accept complimentary privileges in a famous country club were intended to convey moral lessons not only to the persons directly concerned, but to all officialdom as well." He had been nearly as unconventional as Roosevelt, but in a quiet way. When he wanted to address the members of Congress he went to the Capitol and delivered a message in person; when he wanted to speak to individual members of the House and Senate he dropped in to see them, as one neighbor might another neighbor, until he discovered that the press of business at his end of Pennsylvania Avenue prevented him from spending much time at the other end.

"Presidents have to play as well as work," Leupp wrote, "and they have different ways of going about both occupations." Roosevelt had only a general daily program, which he revised at will, but when the clock struck four he closed up shop and started off for two or three hours' exercise—tennis, hiking, riding, boxing, or wrestling. Taft let his visitors take all the time they wanted, but in the late afternoon, when he tired of callers, he would go for a walk or a ride, or head for the golf course. Walking and riding were measures of discipline that he applied to himself. Golf he loved. Had circumstances made it possible, he would have spent most of his time on the golf course.

Wilson, according to Leupp, adopted a routine different from that of both of his predecessors. Mornings he devoted to receiving visitors by appointment. With a few exceptions, no one could have more than five minutes of his time. In the afternoon he secluded himself in order to take care of paper work. Promptly at four he too stopped for the day—to play golf whenever the weather was suitable, or to take a fast spin in his own car, or to stroll through the sleazy sections of Washington, usually unrecognized.

Hunting and fishing, so avidly pursued by Roosevelt, had no appeal for Wilson. He cared nothing about horses. The theater, comedy especially, appealed to him. He liked music. When he read for relaxation he turned to detective stories. Once in his life he started to smoke a cigar, but he threw it away after a few puffs.

The persons who gathered at the White House for a handshake usually got that and nothing more. Roosevelt tried to think up a special greeting for everyone introduced to him, and generally succeeded. Taft liked to repeat names and hold up the line for frequent pleasantries. Wilson walked briskly from one visitor to another, shaking the outstretched hands in silence.

Leupp characterized the Presidents he had known according to their most conspicuous traits. Cleveland he called "the immovable," McKinley "the receptive," Roosevelt "the inventive," Taft "the judicial." Wilson he designated as "the waiting President." At the outset of his administration he had called Congress into special session to carry out the promises of the Democratic platform; since that time he had refused to countenance an adjournment until the most important objectives had been achieved.

"President Wilson is an idealist, a man with a mission," Leupp wrote. "Although men with missions are commonly believed to lack a sense of humor, Wilson contrives to season his idealism with a lot of fun. Even when he is discussing the most serious problems which confront him in office, he cannot keep back a good story if it happens to fit the case in hand."

In no respect had recent Presidents differed more, Leupp believed, than in their attitude toward newspaper publicity. Cleveland hated it. Like Benjamin Harrison, a very modest man, Cleveland communicated with the press through his secretary. McKinley gave the appearance of reticence, but contrived to disseminate such news as he thought would serve the ends of his administration. Roosevelt cultivated correspondents and was always available to them. Taft froze out all except two or three old newspapermen who had been friends of long standing.

Wilson had inaugurated a new regime in dealing with the press. This was to call the correspondents together twice a week for an informal talk, encouraging them to

THE DOVE OF PEACE

Life

Bryan bringing everlasting peace

THE TURKEY TROT OR TANGO ARE LESS OBJECTIONABLE WHEN DANCED BY THE PROPER PEOPLE

One view of the new dances *Life*

Shade of Martha Washington: GRACIOUS! HAS THE MINUET COME TO THIS?

Her husband might have liked it *Life*

Punch, London

Ragtime: an American export to Great Britain

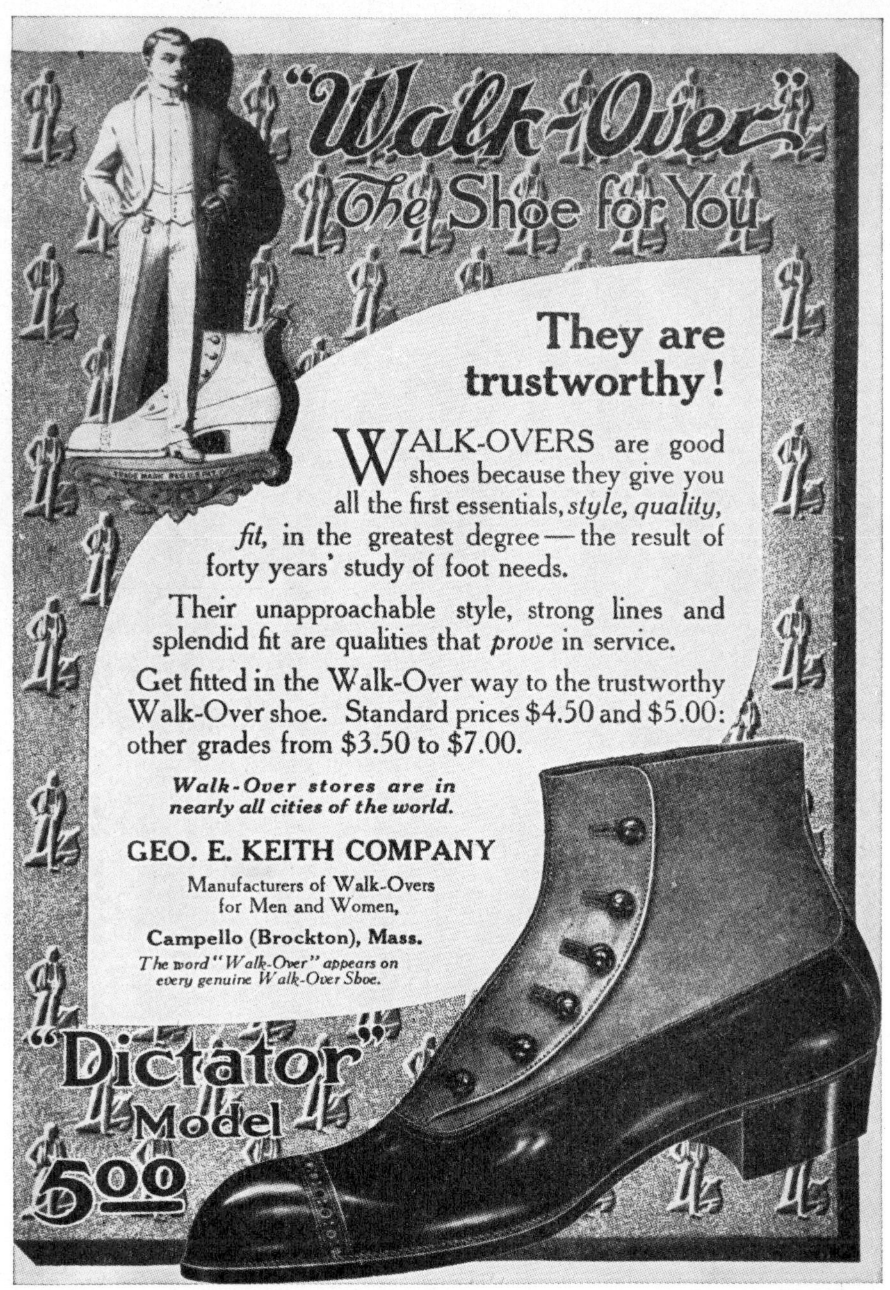

Literary Digest

For the man who wanted to be in style, and could afford it

Donchester
An ARROW
Evening SHIRT

WITH pique or plain patented bosoms, put on the body of the shirt in such a way that no matter what position the wearer may assume, the bosom remains flat and in its place.

$2.00
and up

CLUETT, PEABODY & CO., INC., *Makers of* ARROW COLLARS, TROY, N.Y.

Literary Digest

For the man who wanted to be in high style, and could afford it

Sears Roebuck Catalog

Sears Roebuck styles in men's suits

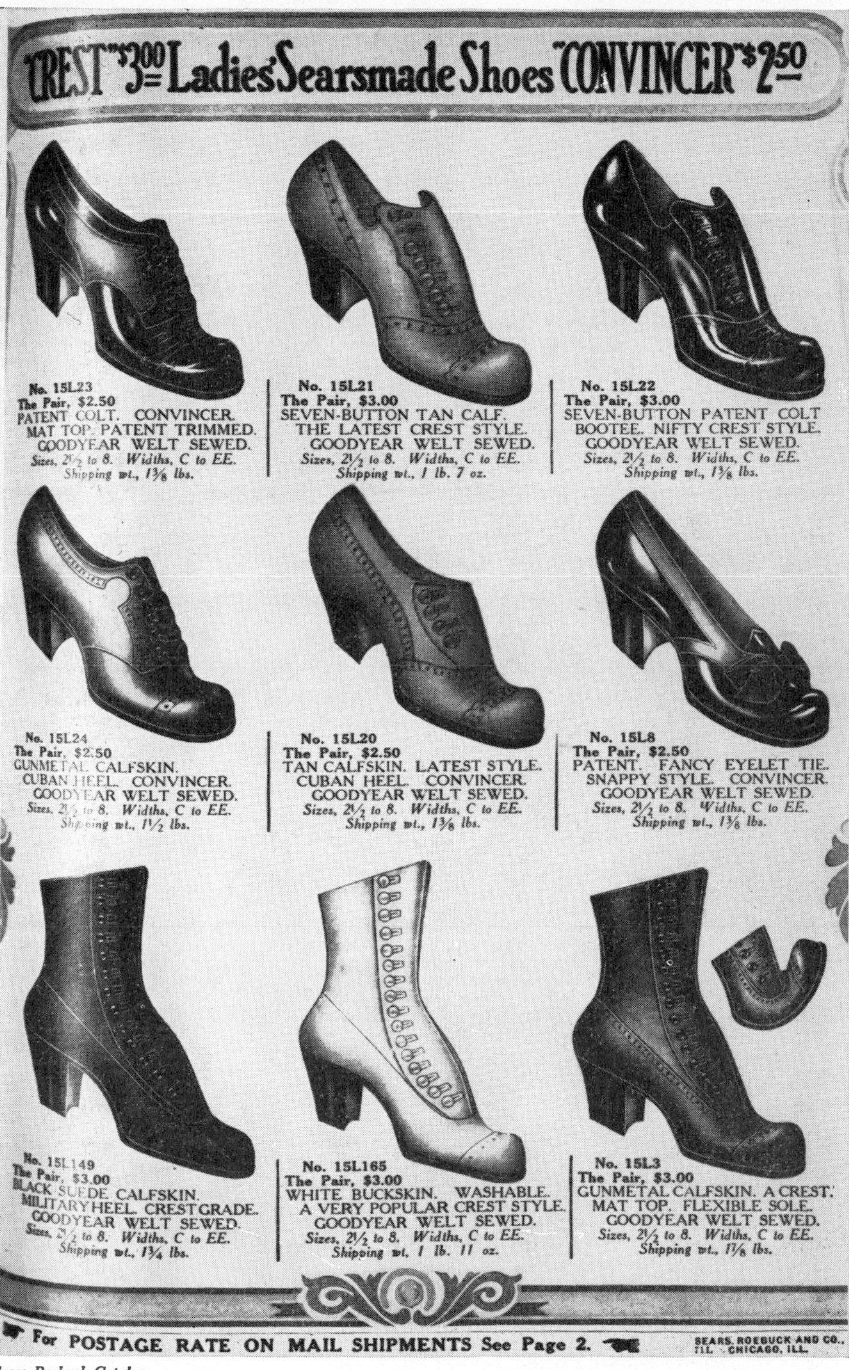

Sears Roebuck Catalog

The shoes that women wore

Ladies Home Journal

Proper dresses in the eyes of the President's daughters

AIRING HER VIEWS

Life

Some women had other ideas

"ZACHARIAH! REMEMBER YOU CAN'T SWIM."

Life

The bikini of 1913

Navy Dept. Photo, National Archives

U.S.S. Texas. Two of these a year, or one, or none?

Brown Brothers

Confederate veterans arriving at Gettysburg for the reunion

Brown Brothers

Union and Confederate veterans in the uniforms they wore at Gettysburg in 1863

Daily News Photo, Chicago Historical Society

Theodore Roosevelt, still the idol of millions

Daily News Photo, Chicago Historical Society

Jess Willard, heavyweight "white hope"

Daily News Photo, Chicago Historical Society

Jack Johnson, heavyweight champion of the world

Brown Brothers

Bryan before Chautauqua audience

The Independent

Something could be said for the income tax

Daily News Photo, Chicago Historical Society

City traffic, Michigan Avenue, Chicago

Kaufmann Fabry Photo, Chicago Historical Society

City traffic, State Street, Chicago

Culver Pictures, Inc.

Rival managers, John J. McGraw of the Giants and Connie Mack of the Athletics, at the opening game of the world series

Daily News Photo, Chicago Historical Society

The "$100,000 infield" of the Philadelphia Athletics: Baker, Barry, Collins, and McInnes

Daily News Photo, Chicago Historical Society

Christy Mathewson ("Big Six") of the Giants. The greatest pitcher of all time?

U. S. Signal Corps Photo, National Archives

Would the "calvary," as the horse soldiers called it, cross the Mexican border?

Daily News Photo, Chicago Historical Society

Jane Addams, extreme right, in a suffrage demonstration.
Chicagoans called her "the sweetheart of humanity."

Punch, London

An English view of Wilson's Mexican policy

Daily News Photo, Chicago Historical Society

Frieda Hempel, opera star

Daily News Photo, Chicago Historical Society

Louisa Tetrazzini, opera star. They all had heft

Daily News Photo, Chicago Historical Society

Lina Cavaliere and Lucien Muratore, opera singers

Chicago Tribune

Wilson begins a year-end vacation

ask any questions they chose. "It is a unique spectacle that the executive office presents on these occasions," Leupp wrote. "The room is circular in shape, and the President's desk is set a little nearer the windows than the center. Behind the desk stands his chair, and behind that Mr. Wilson, his spare figure clad in a simple sack suit of gray tweed. His shoulders have a slight professorial stoop, which is accentuated by his pose as he rests his palms on the back of the chair and lets his body sway a trifle to this side or that when he wishes to emphasize some point or to address some particular member of the human crescent facing him. The meetings last anywhere from ten minutes to twenty."

In short, Wilson had devised the presidential press conference.

This, then, was the man who, on December 2, appeared at the Capitol to fulfill the constitutional obligation of giving the Congress "information of the State of the Union." By this time the appearance of the President in person had become a matter of course. The chamber and the galleries were filled, but the air of excitement that had marked April 8 was missing.

After promising detailed reports by department heads on government operations, the President warmed up to his subject. "The country, I am thankful to say, is at peace with all the world, and many happy manifestations multiply about us of a growing cordiality and sense of community of interest among the nations, foreshadowing an age of settled peace and good will." More and more nations were showing a willingness to arbitrate their differences, and no fewer than thirty-one, representing four-fifths of the population of the world, had signified their assent, in principle, to the negotiation of the new treaties of arbitration which the Department of State had proposed early in the administration.

"There is but one cloud upon our horizon," the President continued. That was Mexico. "There can be no certain prospect of peace in America," Wilson asserted, "until General Huerta has surrendered his usurped authority . . . until it is understood on all hands, indeed, that such pretended governments will not be countenanced or dealt with by the Government of the United States. We are the friends of constitutional government in America; we are more than its friends, we are its champions; because in no other way can our neighbors, to whom we would wish in every way to make proof of our friendship, work out their own development in peace and liberty."

Mexico, the President declared, had no government. The military despotism in Mexico City had no more than "the semblance of national authority." It was doubtful whether the most elementary rights of the Mexican people or of foreigners resident there could be safeguarded. Yet there was some hope. Huerta had forfeited the support even of those who were once his friends. "Little by little he has been completely isolated. By a little every day his power and prestige are crumbling and the collaspe is not far away. We shall not, I believe, be obliged to alter our policy of watchful waiting. And then, when the end comes, we shall hope to see constitutional order restored in distressed Mexico by the conduct and energy of such of her leaders as prefer the liberty of their people to their own ambitions."

Turning to domestic affairs the President urged speedy passage of the currency bill, a measure facilitating farm credit, stronger antimonopoly legislation (on which he promised a special message), a system of presidential primaries (this was unexpected), and an employers' liability act for railway employees.

The nation's territories were on his mind and conscience. Puerto Rico, Hawaii, the Philippines, were ours, indeed, but not ours to do with as we pleased. Such territories, once regarded as mere possessions, were no longer to be selfishly exploited; they belonged to the domain of public conscience and of serviceable and enlightened statesmanship. "We must administer them for the people who live in them and with the same sense of responsibility to them as toward our own people in our domestic affairs." The President believed that Puerto Rico and the Hawaiian Islands could be bound to the United States "by ties of justice and interest and affection," but the Philippines presented a more difficult problem. "We must hold steadily in view their ultimate independence, and we must move toward the time of that independence as steadily as the way can be cleared and the foundations thoughtfully and permanently laid."

Alaska called for special attention. There the nation faced a double duty. The people of Alaska should be given full territorial government as soon as possible, and the territory, "as a storehouse, should be unlocked." This meant the construction of a system of railroads and the erection of ports and terminals, all at government expense. Other resources must be used, "but not monopolized upon any narrow idea of individual rights as against the abiding interests of communities."

In closing, the President asked rhetorically: "May I not express the very real pleasure I have experienced in co-operating with this Congress and sharing with it the labors of common service to which it has devoted itself so unreservedly during the past seven months of uncomplaining concentration upon the business of legislation? Surely it is a proper and pertinent part of my report on 'the state of the Union' to express my admiration for the diligence, the good temper, and the full comprehension of public duty which has already been manifested by both the Houses; and I hope that it may not be deemed an impertinent intrusion of myself into the picture if I say with how much and how constant satisfaction I have availed myself of the privilege of putting my time and energy at their disposal alike in counsel and in action."

Rounding up press opinion, *The Literary Digest* concluded, from correspondents as well as editorials, that the message was received by the Congress "with a cordiality and enthusiasm that lend support to the rumors of an 'era of good feeling' among the political factions in Washington. From the leaders on both sides come tributes to the broad statesmanship of the President's address."

Editors were generally complimentary, even eulogistic. "It heartens, it animates, it stimulates—it soothes," the *New York Herald* declared. "Neither a call to arms, an apology, nor a challenge," said the *Newark News,* but "just that sort of a statement which the head of a great business might issue to his associates in the enterprise regarding the coming year's program and policies." The *New York Journal of Commerce* praised the message as calm and conciliatory, "so suave and smooth and cheerful that one finds it hard to complain of its lack of real analysis or discussion of anything." The President, the *Philadelphia Telegraph* commented, by not committing himself to detail left little chance for dispute, but the message was "reassuring."

On specific subjects, comment varied. To the Springfield (Mass.) *Republican* Wilson's Mexican policy was "in line with the doctrines of the fathers, and in the long run will prove to be the principle to tie to." But the *New York Evening Sun* saw in it only "a dangerous optimism." The *Philadelphia Inquirer* called watchful waiting "just no policy at all. And all the world," the editor concluded, "holds it sides and laughs."

Editorials signaled that the President would have trouble with his proposal for presidential primaries. The *Baltimore News* did not believe that the country was "ready either for surrender of the States' right to regulate or provide for primaries as they will, or for restriction of the parties' right to mold their conventions according to their own ideas of propriety." But the *New York Herald* spotted the basic problem: "A Federal primary law is a certain precursor of a Federal election law. And with the Federal election law what will become of the now winked-at disfranchisement of negro voters in the Southern States?" But on the whole, the country approved.

Mr. Dooley, who reflected public opinion more accurately than most editors, made that fact clear:

"It was a fine message. Th' Dock is not as voluminyous, as Hogan says, as Tiddy Rosenfelt. In th' first place, he can on'y write with wan hand, an' in th' nex' place, d'ye mind, he had to read it himself. Yes, sir; it's a gran' message. Th' grammar ain't bad an' th' punchuation is beyond th' attack iv a scurrilous minority. I wud call it a refined message which cud be played on th' harp.

"In a gin'ral way I gathered that th' Dock is pretty well satisfied with th' prisint administhration so far. He didn't commit himself, mind ye, but it was plain that it had done nawthin' that he felt called on to criticise up to date. It had secured an agreement fr'm th' powers that war was a hellish thing an' proposed to build enough battleships to knock th' head off iv anny power that changed its mind. Th' thrusts must be suppressed with a firm but gentle hand, an' something must be done to make it aisy f'r th' polis to tell a business man fr'm a burglar without th' aid iv thumb marks. . . .

"But Dock Wilson looks f'r no throuble. Says he: 'I have niver injyed an administhration so much. The climate in Wash'nton I find more jovial thin that iv Princeton. Business is excellent. Collections ar-re good. I get me eighty-three thirty-three thirty-three reg'lar on th' first iv th' month. So I bid you ajoo, hopin' I have said nawthin' that wud let you know what I'm goin' to do ontil we meet again.' "

One group definitely not pleased by the President's Annual Message was the National Suffrage Association, meeting in Washington at the time. Suffrage leaders had hoped that Wilson would recommend a constitutional amendment granting the vote to women, but he had not even alluded to the subject.

In the convention a resolution was introduced immediately: "Resolved, That it is the sense of this meeting that President Wilson failed to rise to the sublimest height of democracy when he failed in his message to Congress today to recommend the freedom of half the citizens of the United States and probably half the citizens of the civilized world."

Dr. Anna Howard Shaw, president of the Association, supported the resolution in a speech in which she said: "While President Lincoln had the opportunity of freeing a race President Wilson had the opportunity which might ultimately have meant the enfranchisement of one-half of the human family." Mrs. Carrie Chapman Catt, president of the International Woman's Suffrage Alliance, called Wilson's omission "a great political mistake."

The suffragettes determined to force the President to come out for or against woman suffrage. On December 8 they organized a march to the White House. One hundred militant women marched in a column of two's, headed by Doctor Shaw and Miss Alice Paul, chairman of the congressional committee, who rode in an automobile, and by Mrs. Medill McCormick and Mrs. Desha Breckenridge on foot.

At the White House Doctor Shaw made a short address. She urged the President to recommend a constitutional amendment in a special message, or failing that, to take up the subject in his next regular message. If he were unwilling to do either, would he use his influence to bring about the appointment of a special committee on woman suffrage in the House of Representatives? Doctor Shaw pointed out that "many women have cast their ballots for the president already and have an influence in the government and can affect the government, and do affect it."

Wilson sparred. As governor of New Jersey, he said, he had made a rule which he had continued to follow in the Presidency. He would not urge on Congress "policies which had not had the organic consideration of those for whom he stood as spokesman." In plain language, he would not go beyond the platform on which he was elected, and that platform had contained nothing about woman suffrage. It was impossible for him to speak as an individual: in his office he was not a free man.

On all matters outside the platform, he continued, he was glad to be consulted by members of Congress, and felt honored when they consulted him. One member of the Rules Committee had asked him what he thought about the appointment of a woman suffrage committee in the House, as had already been done in the Senate, and he had replied that he thought it a proper step to take.

The delegates knew very well that the President's answer was specious: the absence of a plank for nation-wide presidential primaries in the Democratic platform had not prevented him from advocating this innovation in his message. But they had found out where he stood, and had to be content.[1]

---

[1] *Arthur Link writes: "Actually, in 1913 and 1914 Wilson believed that the world would be a better place if women stayed in the home." But in 1915, when a suffrage amendment came before the voters of New Jersey he endorsed it.*

The Nineteenth Amendment to the Constitution, conferring the vote on women, was proposed by Congress on June 4, 1919. Ratification was completed on August 18, 1920.

The women who wanted the vote considered the support of the President essential to success; the prohibition forces, in high gear in the fall of 1913, decided to work directly on Congress.

On October 23 the world assembly of the Woman's Christian Temperance Union met in Plymouth Church, Brooklyn, for the first of three conventions of critical importance in the movement for the abolition of the liquor traffic. Representatives from every state in the Union and from nearly fifty foreign countries filled the auditorium. The congregation sang "All Hail the Power of Jesus' Name," then took part in an hour of prayer and testimony on the theme, "Our Help is in the Lord, Which Made Heaven and Earth." The morning session closed with the "Doxology" and a benediction.

Devotions were resumed in the afternoon with an hour of religious instruction in which these questions were considered: How reconcile the sorrows of life, especially such disasters as the loss of the *Titanic,* with God's love and providence? How bring much of the teaching of the Bible into harmony with the inequalities of life? What has modern study done for the Bible? What do we know of the future life?

Reports from around the world brought out interesting facts. South Africa had 2,000 members; Japan, 3,500; Great Britain, 165,000; Italy, 32 (all in one union at Milan). Impressive appeals for aid came from Rhodesia, "where liquor drinking is being introduced"; from China, "where more opium fields have been uprooted than ever before, but where drink is taking the place of opium";

from India, "where Christianity is associated with the liquor traffic, the heathen religions forbidding it"; and from Madagascar, "where the French government opposes temperance work and drink is sadly increasing in the cities."

The most glowing report came from the United States, "the backbone of the world's union," with 250,000 active members, forty working departments, and nine solid prohibition states. Long cheers greeted a proposal for a national prohibition law and an allusion to the "dry" banquets in the White House.

In the evening 1,500 delegates attended a reception at the Hotel Astor in New York. "No more brilliant social function has ever been held by the white ribbon host in this country," the *Northwestern Christian Advocate* asserted. No newspaper, to my knowledge, sent a reporter to interview the hotel bartenders.

In the course of the six-day session the delegates passed dozens of resolutions. One called on the Protestant Episcopal Church to use unfermented wine at the sacrament of the Lord's Supper; another petitioned steamship companies to stop the sale of liquor on passenger liners. Still others dealt with such diverse subjects as Sunday schools, peace and arbitration, school savings, dietary reform, penal reform, charitable work, eugenic marriage, and sterilization of the unfit.

Woman suffrage came in for considerable attention, since most prohibitionists believed that when women were given the vote they would get rid of the saloon in a hurry. Dr. Franklin W. Hooper, Director of the Brooklyn Institute of Arts and Sciences, aroused great enthusiasm when he declared: "It would be a brave man who could stand here and not favor woman suffrage; you will soon be full-fledged citizens." Dr. Anna Howard Shaw deplored the violence of the English suffragettes. Because the leaders of the American movement had abstained from militancy "the American man is always glad to receive us courteously and listen to our arguments. But he always votes us down. The foolish part of the American man is that he thinks we will stop before we get the vote." At one point in the proceedings a score of women from suffrage states marched to the platform singing "We Are the Woman Voters" to the tune of "The Battle Hymn of the Republic." After forming a line across the proscenium each woman told how her state had won the vote. The audience sang "We're Out for Woman Suffrage" to the music of "Dixie."

The convention closed with prayers and the singing of "The Star-Spangled Banner" and "God Be with You till We Meet Again."

From Brooklyn most of the delegates proceeded to Asbury Park for the fortieth annual convention of the National Woman's Christian Temperance Union.

Although the Asbury Park meeting opened with prayers and the singing of hymns, those in attendance devoted more time to business and less time to devotions than they had at Brooklyn. Mrs. Lillian M. N. Stevens, the national president, proudly summarized the progress the Union had made since the Centennial Year of 1876, when it had last met in New Jersey. At that time only twenty-three states had been organized. New Jersey then had fourteen local unions; now it had 300. New York's thirty-seven unions had grown in number to 975. She regretted that New Jersey was still "in bondage to the licensed liquor traffic," and she hoped that the national convention would hasten the time when the state would "outlaw the manufacture and sale of strong drink, and so help to usher in the day of national constitutional prohibition."

Mrs. Stevens wanted no one to be in doubt about the purpose of the Union. "Please note that it is not alone the saloon but the liquor traffic we seek to destroy. The W.C.T.U. is anti-liquor making, anti-liquor importing, anti-liquor selling in saloon, hotel, club, public house, private house, on railroad, on shipboard, in the Gothenburg Dispensary, or any other place by whatsoever name it may be called. We make no distinction between distilled or fermented or malt liquors."

Another speaker, Mrs. Mary Harris Armor, characterized as "The Georgia Cyclone," defined alcohol to a cheering audience. "We know by absolute, incontrovertible twentieth century science that alcohol, to use the language of Dr. Henry Smith Williams, 'is, considering its ultimate effects on the human system, incomparably the most virulent and far-reaching poison known to the medical world,' and that it has the same power to create a progressive appetite for itself that morphine and cocaine have.

"We know," the Georgia Cyclone continued, "that it is preeminently a brain poison, and that it first and most disastrously poisons that part of the brain wherein reside reason, conscience, judgment and self-control, and consequently, alcohol is lowering the physical, mental, and moral standing of the whole human race. . . . When the human race understands the nature of alcohol . . . they will no more consent to alcohol shops wherein this deadly, narcotic-irritant, brain poison is dispensed in highballs, cocktails, and mint juleps, than they will consent to opium dens and cocaine joints."

In the course of the convention the delegates passed resolutions advocating the placing of temperance books in all public libraries, opposing the restoration of the sale of liquor at army posts, urging that liquor be banned from the grounds of the Panama Exposition (to open at San Francisco in 1915), petitioning steamship companies to stop selling liquor on shipboard, and advocating legislation closing the United States mails to liquor advertising.

Like the Brooklyn convention, that at Asbury Park closed with the delegates, hand in hand, singing "God Be with You till We Meet Again."

The real power in the prohibition movement was paraded ten days later when the national convention of the Anti-Saloon League of America assembled at Columbus, Ohio. Opening speakers foreshadowed the primary purpose of the convention and the methods by which that purpose was to be realized. Dissatisfied with its long-established policy of confining the liquor traffic by local option, the Anti-Saloon League was about to embark on a new course. "We are ready to concede," Bishop Luther R. Wilson (Methodist) of New York admitted, "that prohibition in one county does not quite prohibit while the adjacent county is open to the traffic. We must extend the zone of prohibition. Prohibition does not altogether prohibit in one state while the state adjacent is open to the traffic." The answer was obvious: "outlawry of the traffic in strong drink by constitutional amendment."

Governor Ben W. Hooper of Tennessee specified the means that would be used to achieve this end. "The plan is not original," he said. "We copied it from the liquor people. We observed that they owed no ironclad allegiance to any party organization. We have won by giving our candidates the nominations of both the Republicans and the independent Democrats. It is a very comfortable feeling to have two nominations when one runs for office." Put more broadly, the Anti-Saloon League was in politics up to its shoulders and intended to throw the weight of its members and sympathizers behind any candidate who would vote dry, regardless of party affiliation.

Wayne B. Wheeler, superintendent of the Anti-Saloon League of Ohio, also specified the goal upon which the leaders had agreed. "We are launching tonight the most beneficent and far-reaching movement since the Civil War. A great national evil has been localized and quarantined. Over two-thirds of the saloons in America are now in ten states. It took eighty-five years to amend the Constitution of the United States to elect senators by direct vote. It will take but a fraction of that time to make this a saloonless nation."

The men guiding the convention were intensely practical, but as long as the "gaze and thought" were focused on Washington, they could allow the gathering to take on aspects of an old-fashioned Methodist revival. It did. Among those who offered testimony was the Rev. James B. Merwin, eighty-six years old, of Middlefield, Connecticut. Merwin recounted two conversations he had had with Abraham Lincoln during the Civil War. In one Lincoln had said:

"Merwin, we have cleaned up, by the help of the people, a colossal job. Slavery is abolished. The next great question will be the overthrow of the legalized liquor traffic. And you know, Merwin, that my head and my heart, my hand and my purse will go into that work. In 1842, less than a quarter of a century ago, I predicted that the day would come when there would be neither a slave nor a drunkard in the land. I have lived to see one prediction fulfilled. I hope to see the other realized."

Merwin asked whether he could make the statement public. "Yes," Lincoln replied, "publish it as wide as the daylight."

Merwin also related that he had been present when Lincoln and Salmon P. Chase, Secretary of the Treasury, discussed a revenue act levying a tax on distilled spirits. Lincoln had said: "I would rather sever my right hand than sign a bill which would perpetuate the liquor traffic for a single day." "We must have the revenue in this crisis," Chase had replied, "so we must levy revenue on good and evil until the war is finished." Lincoln signed the bill, but with the avowal that he would do everything in his power to repeal it as soon as the war ended.

The delegates greeted Merwin's testimony with wild applause. Hundreds crowded the platform to congratulate him and to obtain his autograph.

(Competent Lincoln students long ago concluded that Merwin was an old windbag whose reports of his conversations with Lincoln had little if any basis in fact.)

Another dramatic episode took place on the second day of the convention when 300 boys of the Lincoln-Lee Legion, a junior organization, all carrying the Stars and Stripes and headed by a drum corps, marched to the platform. Every man and woman in the audience arose; the organ and the assembly rolled forth the hymn, "All Hail the Power of Jesus' Name." As the boys responded to questions asked by the Rev. Dr. Howard H. Russell, founder of the League, "the curtain which had been drawn on one of the west windows in the balcony to shade the eyes of the men on the platform was blown aside by the breeze and a brilliant shaft of light, like a flood of gold, fell across the stage and the little men upon it."

The climax of the meeting came on the afternoon of the third day, November 13, when former Governor J. Frank Hanly of Indiana read the report of the resolutions committee. After reciting that the liquor traffic was "a federal evil, a national menace, too powerful for state authority"; that it dominated parties and conventions and made cowards of public officials; that is claimed the right "to infract municipal ordinances at will . . . and to set aside the constitutional provisions of sovereign states," the report concluded:

"We therefore declare for its national annihilation by an amendment to the federal constitution which shall forever inhibit throughout the territory of the United States the manufacture and sale, and the importation, exportation and transportation of intoxicating liquors to be used as a beverage. To the consummation of this high purpose, we hereby pledge, as pledged our patriot fathers 137 years ago for the nation's independence, 'Our lives, our fortunes and our sacred honor.' "

Cheers rocketed through the hall. When they finally subsided the Rev. Dr. A. M. Courtenay of Columbus, chairman of the resolutions committee, moved the adoption of the report. Mrs. F. D. Richards seconded the motion in the name of the Ohio W.C.T.U. Again 3,500 men and women cheered and shouted and waved arms and handkerchiefs while the organist, all stops out, played "America." The tumult subsided to allow Bishop W. F. Anderson of Cincinnati to offer a prayer consecrating the battle against the forces of evil. Then all joined in the "Doxology."

"On to Washington!" the *Northwestern Christian Advocate* proclaimed in its first issue after the Columbus convention. "The bugle sounds. Every man to arms!"

On to Washington it was. On December 10 one thousand men of the Anti-Saloon League swung along Pennsylvania Avenue toward the Capitol singing "Onward, Christian Soldiers" as they marched. At the Peace Monument a thousand women representing the W.C.T.U. joined them. After the combined force had assembled on the east steps of the Capitol the Rev. Purley A. Baker, general superintendent of the Anti-Saloon League, presented the resolutions passed at the Columbus convention to Senator Morris Sheppard of Texas and Representative Richard Pearson Hobson of Alabama. As soon as the gathering dispersed, both men introduced a prohibitory amendment in their respective houses.[1]

As the year came to its end two dreary strikes, both of long duration, dragged along without prospect of settlement. One had kept the Colorado Fuel and Iron Company, owned by the Rockefeller family, shut down since early August.

---

[1] *The Eighteenth Amendment, inaugurating prohibition, was passed by both houses of Congress in 1917 and ratified on January 13, 1919. It was repealed on December 5, 1933, by the ratification of the Twenty-first Amendment.*

In the Colorado coal field trouble had been brewing for a decade. In 1903 the United Mine Workers of America had led a strike for higher wages and the eight-hour day. The operators, with the aid of the state militia, broke both the strike and the union.

The United Mine Workers came back early in 1913 and organized most of the men, who demanded recognition of the union, a 10 per cent increase in wages, the discharge of armed mine guards, and the right to choose their own boarding houses and doctors. In early August, after the operators refused to meet with union representatives, the men walked out. The companies brought in hundreds of armed guards and evicted the strikers from company houses. The men established tent colonies and settled down for a long test of strength.

The situation remained quiet until mid-October, when a skirmish between guards and miners took place near one of the tent colonies. The guards retired, but soon came back in armored automobiles and machine-gunned the tents. One man was killed, a boy wounded. A few days later guards fired into a mass meeting of strikers, killing three men and wounding a fourth.

On October 26 Governor Ammons called out the entire Colorado National Guard, stationing them throughout Huerfano and Los Animas counties in the southern part of the state. At first the miners were inclined to welcome the guardsmen: they expected them to be easier to get along with than the mine guards. When the militiamen showed that they intended to protect strikebreakers and intimidate the union miners, sentiment changed.

The people in the coal counties lived under constant fear of violence. On December 18 the Colorado State

Federation of Labor met at Denver in a convention called for the purpose of exposing the brutalities of the militia. At the governor's request, the president of the Federation appointed an investigating committee. The committee charged that the adjutant general was unfit for command, that many of the militiamen were former mine guards, and that they were little more than the armed police of the operators. The committee sent its findings to Colorado's Senators and Representatives in Washington and appealed for a federal investigation.

Thus the situation stood at the end of the year.[1]

The second strike, longer, bitterer, more tragic even than the Colorado coal strike, had begun in the copper country of northern Michigan in July. There, in 1912, the forty-two mines of the district had produced 220,000,000 pounds of copper valued at $33,000,000—a fifth of the country's output. About 15,000 men were employed in normal times. They worked a long day—between ten and eleven hours a shift—as compared to the eight and a half-hour shift of Montana copper miners, yet they made less

[1] *The stalemate continued until spring. On April 20, 1914, a pitched battle took place between guardsmen and the miners of the Ludlow tent colony. When a guardsman was killed the militia raked the tents with machine gunfire, killing a boy. Then they set the tents on fire, smothering eleven children and two women.*

Two days later the miners retaliated. In fighting then and during the next few days several men on both sides lost their lives. Southern Colorado, obviously, had slipped into civil war. On April 29, at the urgent request of the governor, President Wilson sent federal troops to restore peace. He also proposed a settlement which the operators rejected. On December 10 the union called off the strike.

money. The principal grievance of the Michigan miners, however, was not hours or wages but the one-man drill. Introduced in 1907, the one-man drill had practically supplanted the two-man drill by 1913. The new device cut down employment and was much harder to use. "The widow maker," the miners called it.

The Western Federation of Miners had tried repeatedly to organize the Michigan copper mines, but without success. In 1913 conditions seemed favorable. The men were restive, and disposed to make sacrifices for the sake of winning shorter hours and better working conditions. Almost to a man they joined the union. On July 14 a letter went to each mine manager threatening a strike unless, by July 21, the operators scheduled a conference before July 28. The union demanded an eight-hour day, a minimum daily wage of $3.00, and either the abolition of the one-man drill or a substantial wage differential for operating it. The mine owners, who had kept organized labor out for fifty years, ignored the letter. A week later the miners walked out and began picketing.

In spite of the fact that nearly all the underground men had struck, the companies attempted to operate. In anticipation of the strike the board of supervisors of Houghton County, center of the copper district, had imported hundreds of armed guards. The inevitable happened soon: clashes between the strikers and the armed guards, and between the strikers and nonunion men still attempting to work. Governor Ferris called out the entire National Guard, 2,700 strong, and posted the troops throughout the area. In Michigan, unlike Colorado, the guardsmen behaved well. "Their presence has undoubtedly been a large factor in preventing violence," Graham Taylor wrote in *The Survey*. "Their methods, and particularly the excesses of a few individuals such as are always present in any large number of young men, have been vigorously criticized, sometimes justly, by union leaders. But the average striker feels that the soldiers, many of whom are trade-union members, have in general treated them fairly."

Early in September Governor Ferris asked Charles H. Moyer, president of the Western Federation of Miners, to submit a list of conditions on which the strike might be settled. Moyer specified reinstatement of the strikers without discrimination and recognition of the right of the men to join the union, with all other issues to be arbitrated. The companies turned down the offer. Later in the month the U. S. Department of Labor suggested a plan of arbitration. Again the companies refused. It was obvious that the operators intended to break the union once and for all. To this end they were willing to give the men at least part of their demands.

At the end of October they announced that they would introduce the eight-hour day on January 1, 1914, and would re-employ all men except those guilty of violence. At the same time the formation of a Citizens' Alliance, organized for the ostensible purpose of bringing the opposing parties together, was announced. The strikers believed the Alliance to be only a front for the companies and would have nothing to do with it.

Christmas approached, with no end to the strike in sight. On Christmas Eve the women's auxiliary of the Western Federation arranged a children's party at Calumet. By early evening the second-story hall was filled to capacity: this would be the only Christmas celebration most of the youngsters would have. Just as the program was about to begin someone yelled "Fire!" The children panicked, ran for the one narrow stairway—and piled up there. In a few minutes seventy-two died, all from suffocation. There was no fire.

The Citizens' Alliance immediately offered $25,000 for relief. The union spurned the money. Word spread that it was a Citizens' Alliance member who had caused the stampede. A committee from the Alliance called on Moyer at his hotel room in Hancock and demanded that he absolve the Alliance from complicity by accepting its relief fund. He refused, and the committee left. A few minutes later several armed men broke into Moyer's room, beat him senseless, and shot him in the back. Then they dragged him through the streets to the railroad station. There he was accosted by the president of the Calumet and Hecla Company, who hit him in the face and threatened to have him hanged if he should ever return to the copper country. The wounded, beaten man was then put aboard a train for Chicago.

The man who had yelled "Fire!" was never found, and a coroners' jury was unable to fix the blame for the tragedy.[1]

On the day of the Calumet tragedy, Woodrow Wilson, content with a congressional session that had given him a lowered tariff and currency and banking reform, headed

[1] *Late in April, 1914, the union, funds exhausted, capitulated. In fact the men had won all their demands except union recognition.*

with his family for Pass Christian, Mississippi. Most Americans agreed that he deserved a vacation.

In the last long shadows of 1913 critics surveyed the state of the arts. The theater, everyone agreed, had not been in the best of health. For this fact many reasons were advanced.

In the first place, *The Nation* reminded its readers, the theater as an institution had never really impressed itself upon the American public. Occasional plays had become themes for general discussion, but the average theatergoer attended a play, liked it or didn't like it, and let it go at that. The technique of the theater was a matter of concern only to professionals and "highbrows."

Motion pictures were fast becoming of much more immediate meaning to the masses. "The good men and women who are fond of writing on literature and life," *The Nation* commented, "who are devoting themselves to the task of bringing the drama into touch with the life of the people, must be amazed, and slightly chagrined, at the intensity with which the film-play has seized upon the popular imagination. The crowds not only throng to the shows; they talk about them, on street corners, in the cars, and over the hoods of baby carriages." The theater could arouse no such interest.

More practical reasons accounted for at least part of the eclipse of the legitimate stage. Both *Life* and *The Theatre* agreed that facilities had been overbuilt. Belasco, Frohman, Claw and Erlanger predicted disaster unless the rage for building new houses subsided. In New York some of the best theaters, old as well as new, had been dark for long periods; in Chicago the situation was even worse. In smaller cities managers could book only an occasional attraction, and all too often that was one which appealed to the crudest taste.

Cost, augmented by the agency system, was another factor. Perhaps the public would not mind paying $2.50 for a seat if that were the box office price, but try to buy good seats at the box office! They could be had only from an agency, which added a fifty cent fee.

The Theatre blamed part of the lack of patronage on the extravagant tastes of the new youth. Miss Debutante was no longer satisfied with a mere visit to the theater. She expected flowers and an expensive supper which, with the cost of tickets, added up to $20 for an evening. Only a fat wallet could stand that strain.

Life's bored critic commented that in "the gray entirety" of the season's productions there had to be a few bright spots. One such, reviewers agreed, was "Years of Discretion," "a play for the middle-aged who try to force the hand of time's clock backward." "Peg o' My Heart," with Laurette Taylor, won praise from all. "The figure of Peg," Montrose J. Moses wrote in *The Independent,* "a wholesome little girl, quaint and charming, warms the heart. . . . The caddish atmosphere in which Peg finds herself all the more accentuates the appeal of her character, and Miss Taylor acts the part with strokes of genuine art." "Within the Law," by Bayard Veiller, a "crook" play which did not altogether condemn the ethical aberations of some of its characters, proved so popular that six companies were put on the road. John Emerson's "The

Conspiracy" was a good representative of a sure-fire type: the mystery play. Although one reviewer compared it to a "yellow-back novel," two road companies played the country and a third took it to London. "Fine Feathers," by Eugene Walter, which illustrated "the curse of rapid living in New York," showed "a certain conscience" on the part of the dramatist even though much of the melodrama was commonplace and threadbare. Edward Sheldon's "Romance" gave Davis Keane the role of an Italian opera singer in the New York of the 1860's. The play was a success, although critics complained that the author failed to catch the spirit of old New York and allowed his story to degenerate into blatant melodrama. Nothing but good was said of "The Poor Little Rich Girl," by Eleanor Gates, a story of the neglected child of rich parents. "The most refreshing play of fact and fancy seen for many years," Montrose J. Moses wrote in *The American Year Book*.

There were others, of course, notably "A Good Little Devil," "Belasco's contribution to the cycle of fantastical productions" seen early in the year; Frederick Lonsdale's "The Woman of It," a conventional drama of an unhappy marriage, "thoroughly English"; William Collier's "Never Say Die," a farce about a man who failed to die when his physicians had promised he would; Carl Roessler's "Five Frankforters," based upon an episode in the life of the Rothschilds. The Irish Players paid another visit to New York; the English actors Sir Johnston Forbes Robertson and Cyril Maude toured the country; and the Princess Theater experimented with evenings of one-act plays.

But the season was not as dull as the succession of lackluster productions would indicate. Several plays dealing with that bugaboo of the times, white slavery, provided excitement. "The Lure," by George Scarborough, "The Fight," by Bayard Veiller, and "The House of Bondage," by Reginald Wright Kaufman all dealt with commercialized vice. All were presented in New York City, and all were soon closed by Chief Police Magistrate William McAdoo.

McAdoo had encouraged the production of Shaw's "Mrs. Warren's Profession" in New York. In "The Lure" he saw something quite different. "I believe the play to be indecent and immoral," he asserted, "and in part gross and revolting, and that it is entirely covered by Section 1140 of the Penal Law. . . . The play is said to be an exposé of white slavery, and therefore to be used as a valuable preventive against young girls being lured into these traps. . . . We do not need to uncover a sewer to convince people as to its filthiness nor to warn those of ordinary cleanly habits against getting into it."

Lee Shubert, who had produced "The Lure," defended his motives in a letter to the Assistant District Attorney. Before production the manuscript was presented to social workers who without exception endorsed it. After it opened it won the immediate commendation of a number of judges, police officers, and social workers. Many public-spirited citizens had urged Shubert to fight the Chief Magistrate's order, but in view of the sharp division of public opinion he had decided to have the play rewritten to meet the objections that had been lodged against it.

Newspapers and magazines took up the controversy. *The Outlook* agreed that if a play was in fact indecent and immoral it should be suppressed. The trouble came from the difficulty of determining the fact. There was general agreement that Brieux's "Damaged Goods" had not "the slightest effect of rousing evil passion or satisfying prurient curiosity." On the other hand certain "gay" musical comedies, in which no offensive word was spoken, were essentially "salacious and dangerous." But some distinction must be made "between that legitimate use of passion and plain speaking which seriously deals with evil to make it repulsive and a tragic warning, and that use which appeals purposely, and with vile desire to make money, to all that is lowest in human nature."

"Who is to be the judge in these things?" the *Philadelphia Ledger* asked. "That is the crux of the difficulty. A censorship is impossible, for the average result must always be the suppression of the original and the progressive and the sanction of the commonplace and the conventional. It is intolerable that the police or any other such authority should be empowered to pass upon artistic productions of any sort. The surest safeguards are to be found in an enlightened public opinion."

The *New York Times* broadened the field by taking in books and motion pictures as well as the theater. Like the *Ledger,* it placed its reliance upon public opinion. That force, in the case of the controversial plays, had already been effective. Nearly every newspaper in the city had demanded their removal from the stage, and in this demand the papers had the support of "large numbers of reputable citizens." (Who made the count?)

The *Times* concluded: "There has been a great deal of painful and morally degrading discussion of evils which can never be lessened by promiscuous and irresponsible debate. The public movement against these brothel dramas indicates that the people are alive to the dangers of the situation. They have called a halt. Too many abominable books with a pretense of moral purpose have been tolerated.'"[1]

"The world of concert and opera," admitted Arthur Farwell, of *Musical America,* writing in *The American Year Book,* "represents after all but an insignificant proportion of the whole population, from two to five per cent, in American cities." (I can remember only two concerts of consequence presented at about this time in Mansfield, Ohio. One was given by Maud Powell, then nearing the end of a brilliant career as a violinist. The other was a symphony concert—by what orchestra I do not recall. I do remember that the orchestra played in the Congregational Church, wherefore the members had to go outside—it was a hot night—for their beer during the intermission.)

Nevertheless, where concert artists did appear, where opera could be presented, where resident symphony orchestras were established, there was lively interest, and newspapers and magazines devoted far more space to music than the number of readers could have justified.

---

[1] *Censorship, directed at books more often than the theater, is still very much with us. "The censors continued to be active in 1962. Henry Miller's novel,* Tropic of Cancer, *added to its record, established the previous year, of being the most censored book in modern American publishing history. Textbooks and school library books were accused of political and moral subversion in attacks by self-appointed 'experts' whose efforts were disturbingly successful."* Publishers' Weekly, *January 21, 1963.*

Critics—American critics—hoped for the establishment of a "national musical individuality, a condition now reached by various modern nations, though one merely adumbrated in America."

They found some encouragement in 1913 when Edgar Stillman Kelley's Symphony in B minor, "New England," was produced by the Litchfield County Choral Union at Norfolk, Connecticut. "More than interesting," one critic wrote, "worthy of study, and of more than one hearing. Mr. Kelley is not afflicted with 'modernities,' and does not strive, by straining after unusual harmonic (or unharmonic) combinations to cover up a lack of ideas."

At the same festival, in early June, the new "Negro Rhapsody" of Henry Gilbert, who was "striking the lyre with a bolder hand than perhaps any other American," was presented. Musical patriots took hope also from Arne Oldberg's "Symphonic Variations," produced at the North Shore Festival at Evanston, Illinois, with the composer conducting. "Mr. Oldberg's consummate mastery of thematic development," Farwell wrote, "combined with his high sense of beauty and exalted idealism, entitle him to a place among the foremost modern composers."

The year was as notable for the works of European composers performed for the first time in the United States as for new American compositions. The Fourth Symphony of Jean Sibelius, played by the New York Symphony Society in early March, lifted Finland to the rank of a world power in music. "It is a work of extraordinary power and individuality," Farwell wrote, "owing probably even more to the personality of the composer than to the striking national medium through which he works. It is a new voice in music, reflecting nothing of Wagner, Strauss, or Debussy."

Even newer, even more striking, was "Five Small Pieces," by the Viennese futurist Arnold Schoenberg, a work first performed in America by the Chicago Symphony Orchestra on the last day of October. The *Chicago Tribune* reported: "Even the conservative matineé audience, though dazed and astonished, was keenly interested by this most novel and original music. A few enthusiasts ventured to applaud. One objector gave vent to a shrill whistle. Several times the whole audience laughed heartily and somewhat derisively. But the general impressions of the public seemed to be concerned with curiosity, wonder, and perplexity."

But it was opera, rather than concerts, which offered most of the new departures of the year. The Chicago-Philadelphia Opera Company, organized in 1911 to present seasons in both cities, became exclusively a Chicago organization. From the beginning the company had been a kind of stepchild of the Metropolitan, with several Metropolitan directors on its board, and with a general manager, Andreas Dippel, closely allied with Gatti-Casazza. The idea seems to have been that this alliance would keep the Chicago-Philadelphia company from competing with New York for singers. But when the Chicago season began to show a profit, as it did in the third year, and when friction developed between Dippel and Cleofonte Companini, the musical director and conductor, the Chicagoans, led by Harold McCormick of the International Harvester family, bought out the New Yorkers, released Dippel and decided to "make culture hum" on their own. (The phrase was the *Literary Digest's*.)

In New York, two new ventures challenged the prestigious Metropolitan. One came from the fertile brain of the German-born composer, manager, and impresario, Oscar Hammerstein. For many years Hammerstein had aspired to produce opera in English at popular prices. In 1905, to realize this ambition, he had begun the Manhattan Opera House on 34th Street. Before it was completed he decided to make it a rival of the Metropolitan. Early in December, 1906, he opened the house with an extravagant production of Bellini's "I Puritani." For the next three years the two establishments engaged in fierce competition. The pace finally became too fast for Hammerstein. In 1910 he sold his interest in the Manhattan to the Metropolitan for $2,000,000 and agreed not to produce opera in its territory for ten years.

Early in 1913 Hammerstein asked the Metropolitan Opera Company to release him from his agreement: he had taken up again his long-consuming ambition to present opera in English. The Metropolitan directors refused. Whereupon Hammerstein announced that he would establish the American National Grand Opera Company, build a house for it, and not only offer opera in English but compete with the Metropolitan on its own terms. He began construction at Lexington Avenue and 51st Street, and the Metropolitan sought an injunction.

Not trusting completely the processes of the law, the Metropolitan directors decided on a flank attack. The City Club, an organization hitherto devoted to municipal reform, suddenly announced that it would sponsor the Century Opera Company which would produce forty-five weeks of opera in English, French, German, and Italian at prices ranging from 25 cents to two dollars. The Metropolitan had offered to co-operate by lending costumes and scenery, and several of its directors accepted places on the Century board. No knowledgable person could doubt that the Century was the Metropolitan's answer to Hammerstein's challenge.

Hammerstein gave a typical fulmination to the press. The Century people had claimed that they could produce acceptable opera for $13,000 a week. "It cost me $25,000 a week," he said, "and it cost the Metropolitan Opera Company $35,000 a week." To the Metropolitan directors he wrote: "I intended to devote the edifice [his Lexington Avenue Opera house] solely to a permanent institution for grand opera in English at $3 the highest. You, twenty-four hours after my announcement to this effect, announced the creation of another institute [The Century] at $2 the highest. Under the guise of philanthropy, you, nevertheless, solicit alms from the public . . . for nothing else but a sinister scheme to destroy my absolutely financially disinterested efforts in a noble cause. Consequently, I will produce grand opera at certain periods at $1—at others at $6 a seat, in any language excepting one particular one which your conduct deserves, but which is unfit to be printed."

The Century Company began its season at the Century Theater on September 15 with "Aïda." The performance was in Italian the opening night; English was used for the remainder of the week. "La Gioconda," "The Tales of Hoffman," "Lohengrin," "Madame Butterfly," "Tosca," and two or three others were given in this same manner, but before the end of the year the one night a week in the original tongue was abandoned. Fairly large audiences and financial success greeted the venture.

Hammerstein had promised to open on November 24 but had to postpone because of delays in the construction of his building. As the year ended he found himself under an injunction, obtained by the Metropolitan directors, not to produce opera. In 1914 he abandoned the effort and devoted the Lexington to other theatrical uses.

The operatic civil war in New York and the Chicago Opera Company's assertion of independence did not prevent ventures into novelty. On February 9 Chicago gave a premiere performance of "Kuhreigen," by William Kienzl. The *Chicago Tribune's* critic, attuned to the moral temper of the times, wrote that "such words as decadent, degenerate, neurotic, perverse, cacophonous, discordant, uncouth, and ugly, may be given a well earned rest while it is attempted to praise in old fashioned phrase the homely virtues of romance and sentiment, of simple, pastoral melody, of dainty dance and graceful song."

(As far as I have been able to ascertain, the opera has not been heard of since, and the composer's name is not to be found in the standard music reference books.)

Two weeks later the Metropolitan introduced a new opera, "Cyrano," by Walter Damrosch, the conductor of the New York Symphony Society. The critic of the *New Music Review* wrote of the composer: "His score is commendable for its coloring, its richness, and for the sure touch with which he has emphasized and elucidated passages now emotional, now gay, now picturesque, now tragic." But, the writer concluded, the opera "cannot be called music of inspiration, of originality, or in the highest sense, of power"—a verdict which posterity has endorsed by consigning it to the dust bin.

Moussorgsky's "Boris Godunoff," which the Metropolitan offered to New York on March 19, turned out to be of a different order. Although not new—it had been staged in St. Petersburg as early as 1874—it was a departure from the familiar pattern. In it, one reviewer said, the composer had relied so much on folk music that the Russian people spoke for themselves. *The Nation's* critic could not believe that "Boris Godunoff" would prove to be a permanent addition to the Metropolitan's repertory. "The choruses were admirably sung," he admitted, "and under the direction of Mr. Toscanini the orchestra was at its best, but the lack of ingratiating melody will prevent the public from taking this opera to its heart." Arthur Farwell, on the other hand, considered "Boris" an instantaneous success.

In the fall, the Chicago Opera Company gave Massenet's "Don Quichotte" its American premiere at Philadelphia. The score, *Musical America* found, offered "a continuous flow of melody, light, sometimes almost inconsequential, and not often of dramatic significance, but at all times pleasing, of an elegance that appeals to the esthetic sense, and in all its phrases appropriate to the story." The French baritone, Vanni-Marcoux, was effective in the role of Cervantes' befuddled knight-errant; Mary Garden was equally successful as Dulcinea. "A simple and moving story set to very effective music," *Musical America* concluded.

But the high point of the opera season came near the end of the year— on December 9, when the Metropolitan gave the first American performance of Richard Strauss's "Der Rosenkavalier." This story of amorous intrigue in the eighteenth century ran some risk, the moral climate of 1913 being what it was, of censorship. But Henry E. Krehbeil, music critic of the *New York Tribune,* discovered an underlying moral purpose in the comedy which to some extent justified its "frank salaciousness," and the *New York Sun* pointed out, realistically, that most of the people in the audience had no idea what was going on. H. T. Parker of the *Boston Transcript* thought that the opera would be "tonic, broadening and humanizing" because, after all, one "could not live by moral earnestness alone."

The music, one can infer from the reviews, baffled the critics. Several gave it scant attention, "doubtless," the *Literary Digest* surmised, because of "The Straussian polyphony." To *The Independent* waltz themes recurred in abundance in the score, but they were "interrupted, diverted and distorted in true Richard Strauss fashion." Indeed, the whole opera was "a bizarre combination of the smooth Johann Strauss of the waltzes and the anarchistic Richard who deliberately let loose the dogs of war in the orchestral pit!"

The principals of the cast—Otto Goritz, Margarethe Ober, and Frieda Hempel—came in for the highest praise.

In the article which Edward Everett Hale, professor of English at Union College and son of the author of "The Man Without a Country," wrote on American literature for the 1913 edition of *The American Year Book,* he estimated that about 350 works of fiction by American writers had appeared during the year. Novels constituted by far the largest category in the publishers' lists. Hale classified them as works of social significance, as genre pieces (although he did not use the term), and as books of adventure and mystery. Contemporary reviewers, however, had a tendency to distinguish between novels written for entertainment and those which had a more serious purpose. Only by applying some such standards—the separation of the transitory from the significant—can the literary output of 1913 be appraised fifty years afterward.

In truth, that output cannot be ranked very high, although reviewers, on the whole, treated it gently. Experienced practitioners continued to rely on formulas which had long since created substantial bank accounts. Robert W. Chambers published *The Business of Life,* which a reviewer in the *Chicago Tribune* characterized as "virile and absorbing," with a heroine who would take her place "among the most individual heroines of recent years." Randall Parrish's contribution for the year was *The Maid of the Forest,* another excursion into the frontier history which he had learned so well to endow with improbable romance. George Barr McCutcheon produced *A Fool and His Money,* the story of an international marriage which, after various trials, turned out well in the end. (How else, in 1913?) Dodd, Mead and Company, McCutcheon's publishers, showed themselves well aware of shifting currents when they published an advertisement which asked, "What makes McCutcheon readers as numerous as the sands of the sea?" And answered: "Isn't it because his novels are CLEAN, WHOLESOME, OPTIMISTIC, AND INTENSELY INTERESTING?"

Elinor Glyn may have been trying to live down the notoriety with which *Three Weeks* had enveloped her when she came out with *The Point of View.* At any rate her publishers stressed the contention that Mrs. Glyn's performance proved that she could write a book "of the highest ideals and literary distinction." Houghton Mifflin pushed *The Story of Waitstill Baxter* by Kate Douglas Wiggin, author of *Rebecca of Sunnybrook Farm,* as "a novel of rare insight and infinite sweetness." John Fox, Jr. published another story of the mountain people, *The Heart of the Hills,* which even the hard-to-please *Nation* refused to dismiss as another light romance, but commended for the author's ability to enlist sympathy for "his little men and women of the wilderness." Rex Beach offered *The Iron Trail* to a large and uncritical audience, Gene Stratton-Porter gave *Laddie* to many thousands of sentimental women, and Sax Rohmer brought out *The Insidious Dr. Fu Manchu,* which occasioned a sharp criticism, rare even in *The Nation*: "Among the many victims of violence in these chronicles we may mention the rules of English grammar."

Certain novelists came close to works of distinction. Among them were the two Indianans, Booth Tarkington and Meredith Nicholson. Tarkington came out with *The Flirt,* a novel that approached the realism that in a few years would make Sinclair Lewis famous. Nicholson published *Otherwise Phyllis,* a fine portrayal of an Indiana town but with too much "wholesomeness" to endow it with lasting life. In *Westways: A Villiage Chronicle,* which treated the Civil War from the standpoint of a surgeon in the Union army, the physician-novelist S. Wier Mitchell turned out his last and perhaps his best book. The University of Chicago professor Robert Herrick published *One Woman's Life.* Critics could—and did—compare Herrick with Balzac, but like Tarkington, he could not bring himself to the merciless depiction of his characters that might have given him enduring fame.

The novels of the year in which contemporary critics saw enduring worth were few. Edward Everett Hale's candidate for the distinction was *New Leaf Mills,* by William Dean Howells—a judgment doubtless due more to Howell's towering reputation than to the merits of the book. Most reviewers named *The Inside of the Cup,* by Winston Churchill (of Cornish, New Hampshire, U.S.A.), and *V. V.'s Eyes,* by Henry Sydnor Harrison. Of *The Inside of the Cup,* which dealt with Christianity as it was and as it should be, *The Outlook* wrote: "The book has the nobility which comes only from high purpose and perfect sincerity; it has the breadth of interest which Mr. Churchill always gives his fiction; and the love-making, which grows like a flower in a tempest, has a fresh and unhackneyed charm. In the flood of stories of ephemeral interest and relaxing . . . moral quality this novel has the lift and invigorating air of a mountain." *V. V.'s Eyes,* which dealt with the relationship between a dedicated social reformer and a frivolous selfish woman, came in for equally high praise, also from *The Outlook.* "One of the strongest and at the same time most delicately wrought American novels of recent years," the reviewer wrote. "It is, in fact, a high form of praise . . . to say that the novel moves the heart toward social sympathy without being either 'preachy' or platitudinous; and equally high praise to say that the author's treatment of plot and incident is true rather than conventional."

One other novel won approval from a few discerning critics. Of *O Pioneers!,* by Willa Cather, Elia W. Peattie wrote in the *Chicago Tribune*: "A book of more rugged simplicity would be difficult to find." "Few American novels of recent years have impressed us as strongly as this," *The Nation* said. "The sureness of feeling and touch, the power without strain, which mark this book, lift it far above the ordinary product of contemporary novelists."

Of all the novels published in 1913, it is probable that only *O Pioneers!* has an appreciable number of readers today.

In poetry the story was much the same as in fiction. Edward Everett Hale, summarizing, mentioned new collections by Madison Cawein, Bliss Carman, William Rose Benét, Corinne Roosevelt Robinson, and Josephine Preston Peabody—all authentic voices, and all minor. Hale ignored *Poetry: A Magazine of Verse,* which signalized the completion of its first year in the fall of 1913 by awarding two prizes. One, of $250, went to William Butler Yeats for "The Grey Rock"; the other, of $100, was bestowed on Nicholas Vachel Lindsay, of Springfield, Illinois, for "General William Booth Enters Into Heaven," which had appeared in the January, 1913, issue. "A big breezy cheerful troubador this young man," the editor wrote, "who accepts without complaint the modern world's refusal to pay its poets a 'living wage,' quite simply takes us at our own word, and turns beggar that he may effect a free exchange of rhymes for bread. Wholly sturdy and high-hearted is his faith in himself and his town, his brave resolve to leaven our whole lump with a bit of yeast in Springfield. . . . Mr. Lindsay is the real thing."

Robert Frost, who had just completed a year at the State Normal School, Plymouth, New Hampshire, teaching psychology, published his first book of verse, *A Boy's Will.*

The fiction of the year was undistinguished, and poetry saw only two fresh talents emerge, but the authors of non-fiction produced a respectable number of durable works. *The Reminiscences of Augustus Saint-Gaudens,* edited by his son, Homer Saint-Gaudens, appeared; so did John Bigelow's *Retrospections of an Active Life, The Life and Letters of Charles Eliot Norton, The Life and Letters of Gen. G. G. Meade,* and *The Letters, Speeches and Correspondence of Carl Schurz.* Jack London published *John Barleycorn,* a candid recital of his disastrous experiences with alcohol. And Francis Grierson, a musician who had spent his boyhood and youth in pre-Civil War Illinois, brought out *The Valley of the Shadows,* an uneven masterpiece which continues to fascinate readers with its account of prairie life in the shadow of approaching war.

John Bach McMaster finished his eight-volume *History of the People of the United States from the Revolution to the Civil War. The Independent* predicted that he would join the small group of American historians which included Bancroft, Parkman, Rhodes, and Adams. To *The Nation,* McMaster could not be put in the same class with Adams, and he lacked "the poise and personal element of Rhodes." He would rank, nevertheless, "as a highly trained compiler." (Posterity has placed him in between these two estimates, but has tended to lean toward *The Nation's* verdict.) Milo M. Quaife came out with the first of many books, *Chicago and the Old Northwest, 1763-1835,* still the most inclusive and dependable treatment of the subject. Charles A. Beard, then of Columbia, published his iconoclastic *Economic Interpretation of the*

Constitution. "No more important work on the Constitution has appeared," *The Independent* commented—an appraisal that still holds good despite the sniping of historians possessed of no more than a fraction of Beard's erudition and imagination. George Lockhart Rives, a lawyer without "professional" historical training, a handicap fast becoming insurmountable in the eyes of the academicians, was responsible for *The United States and Mexico, 1821-1848,* the first comprehensive account of the subject. *The Nation,* revolting against the snobbery of the graduate schools, commented that it was "a pleasant thing" that human interest was not slighted, and that political and military developments were considered to be as important as the wheat supply. "We have had some excellent writers among the teachers," *The Nation* admitted, but "we have had many who made historical literature a dull and lifeless waste."

Twenty-four-year-old Walter Lippmann published his first book, *A Preface to Politics,* and paid the penalty for cleverness, cynicism, and humor which some reviewers considered unbecoming to his tender years. Yet, *The Nation* remarked, "his characterizations of Roosevelt, Wilson, Bryan, and Tammany Hall are penetrating, and there are occasional vignettes that are worthwhile. For instance: 'From Senator Lodge, for example, we do not expect any new perception of popular need. We know that probably his deepest sincerity is an attempt to reproduce the atmosphere of the Senate a hundred years ago. The manners of Mr. Lodge have that immobility which comes from too much gazing at bad statues of dead statesmen.' For the sake of this kind of thing one can easily pardon his [Lippmann's] rather juvenile and cocksure pronouncements on such things as art, morals, and religion, with the feeling that he will probably outgrow most of them."

If one great book was published in 1913 it was Albert Bigelow Paine's *Mark Twain: A Biography.* Here, wrote William Lyon Phelps in *The Independent,* "we see Mark Twain exactly as he was, childishly angry at being beaten at billiards, horribly profane and sacrilegious, tender, patient and sweet with little children . . . raging with knightly anger at snobbishness, cruelty, extortion, and affectation, speaking his own mind on the great names in letters, and steadily working at his art. The way to judge of the success of a biography is not to estimate the merits of its literary style, but to consider whether or not it gives a vivid, complete and permanent picture of the subject.

"American literature on the whole," Phelps concluded, "has been so second-rate, so uninspired, so full of little men and commonplace works, that we are grateful for so complete and honest a presentation of one of our few world figures."

In view of what was happening in the theater, in dress, popular music, and the dance, it could hardly be expected that books would escape the close scrutiny of the moralists. They didn't. We confine ourselves to Chicago, probably less urbane than New York, but probably more tolerant than Cedar Rapids or Topeka. (I have picked the cities at random, and cannot adduce evidence to support my supposition.) At any rate, in Chicago one could have heard Mrs. Cornelia Baker, in a talk before the Chicago Woman's Club, assail the books of Robert W. Chambers as a menace to the morals of young people. "I know girls," Mrs. Baker said, "who have formed the habit of pouring perfumery over a lump of sugar and eating it, because of a similar habit of one of Chambers' characters, who got into serious trouble because of the habit. All of his women smoke cigarets and drink cocktails. The things his people say and do make up the objectionable features of his books. The stories are not badly told, but it is certainly to be regretted that he does not turn to more wholesome subjects."

Later in the year other speakers before the Chicago Woman's Club resumed the attack. One characterized the new literature as "ragtime turkey trot"; another said that letters in the United States had struck "sex o'clock." Mrs. Edward Theodore Johnson of Oak Park named candidates for a literary blacklist:

Robert Herrick, because he took a malicious pleasure in showing women for what they were.

Winston Churchill who, in *The Inside of the Cup,* had fallen into the "sex snare," and offered a recital of "free love philosophy."

Edith Wharton, one time possessed of a fine style, now succumbed to "the fad of sex."

In concluding the meeting one member called on the Woman's Club to take a firm stand. "The fiction of our day not only is corrupting the imagination of the youth of the present day, but will form a harmful influence upon the next generation. The freedom with which sex is now discussed is responsible for the awful immorality among small children of our time."

Book prices, by the standards of 1963, were low. Novels, usually illustrated, ranged from $1.00 to $1.40; non-fiction from $2.00 to $2.50. Roosevelt's *Autobiography,* a well made volume of 597 pages, was priced at $2.50; Beard's *Economic Interpretation of the Constitution,* 330 pages, sold for $2.25.

But even in 1913 price-cutters, notably R. H. Macy and Company of New York, were busy. For several years Macy's had been selling popular titles below the publishers' prices. The publishers retaliated by refusing to sell to Macy's, and by withholding their books from any jobbers who supplied the firm. Various suits were filed and decided in various ways until the fall of 1913, when the United States Supreme Court ruled that publishers could not lawfully combine to stop the sale of their books at reduced prices. "At first glance," the *Literary Digest* commented, "it might seem that everybody concerned in the making, selling, and buying of books would be happy. . . . The 'consumer' will get his books cheaper and can afford to buy more of them; the retailer will be perfectly free to buy his books at regular wholesale prices from any jobber or publisher, and to sell them at any price which suits his fancy; the publisher will thus sell more books and the author will get bigger royalties."

The *Digest* found that the publishers dissented violently. "They assert that the department stores will be the only winners—the book-buyer will only be helped in buying 'best sellers' and the department-store class of literature; the retailer who cannot meet department-store competition in those lines, and who cannot exist on his sales of works of higher grade, must put up his shutters; the publishers will find no retail outlet for their more serious, slow-selling works, which the book-lover will find it difficult to obtain."

George Haven Putnam, of G. P. Putnam's Sons, put the publishers' case more pungently. "What the dry-goods dealer [Macy's] has in mind is not the distribution of good literature at a lower price than that at which it will be sold by the regular bookseller, but the bringing into a 'state of mind' a customer (and particularly a feminine customer) who, finding that there is a reduction easily calculated on a popular book, convinces herself that the enterprising dry-goods dealers are selling all their "fripperies' at a similar reduction."[1]

---

[1] *Despite a maze of "fair trade" laws and court decisions, publishers have still not been able to do away with price-cutting.*

EPILOGUE

At the beginning of this book I said that I wanted to picture the year 1913 as it unfolded before the eyes of a mature, intelligent, and inquisitive American. In closing the account, I shall draw on the recollections of an American reasonably intelligent, definitely inquisitive, but at the time, far from mature. I shall try to describe certain aspects of middle class living as I remember them, and I shall make a good many statements which, to readers of my own age, will seem to be superfluous. My contemporaries, for example, do not need to be told that there was no radio in 1913 (except for commercial and ship-to-ship communication) but I suspect that this fact will surprise a good many younger readers. And so with many other facilities and conveniences which a generation that did not see them come into existence tends to take for granted.

I lived in a comfortable frame house. Writing, as I am, in bitter winter weather, I am glad to recall that we had central heating—a warm air coal furnace. It was hand-fired, of course—stokers would not come until later, and oil and gas furnaces not until much later. We did not have running hot water, but hot water for baths was supplied by a huge, nickel-plated, gas-fired contrivance above the bathtub that was turned on only when needed.

In 1913 the house was illuminated by gas. Each fixture had to be individually lighted, and a supply of long wax tapers was kept for this purpose. Electricity was available for lighting (except on the farms), and many were using it, but power failures were frequent. Two or three years later, when my father remodeled our house extensively, he put in wiring but retained the gas fixtures. We often needed them.

My mother, like most housewives, cooked on a gas range—a range with the oven above the burners, where it would still be located if designers of appliances had any regard for convenience. In the summer we "took" ice, a luxury in which even many well-to-do families, which we weren't, did not indulge. (I know. In 1918 I spent the first of four summers carrying ice. In the morning my partner and I worked through one of the wealthy sections of town. We carried no more than two-thirds of the houses and the competing company served only a few of the others. In the afternoon our route took us through a working class neighborhood in which about one resident in ten was a customer. There was no mechanical refrigeration.)

In the house we had no electrical appliances—no electric iron, no vacuum cleaner, no toaster, no electric coffeemaker, no electric-powered washing machine, although embryonic versions of all five were on the market. My mother still relied on a heavy solid flatiron heated on the stove, cleaned the rugs with a Bissell carpet sweeper, made toast in the oven and coffee in an enamelware pot, and washed by hand. (Many women used a washing machine which was essentially a covered wooden tub with paddles agitated by a lever which the operator moved back and forth.) The sewing machine was driven by a treadle. Once or twice a year it was kept busy for several days by a seamstress, engaged long in advance, who did the sewing for which a busy mother could not find time.

With few exceptions, usually among the wealthy who owned carriages or automobiles, housewives ordered groceries and meat by telephone, and ordered them from separate stores. Butchers operated their own shops, unaffiliated with groceries. All stores, except dime stores, were independently owned. The one chain food store in Mansfield at this time was the Grand Union and Pacific Tea Company, which limited itself to tea, coffee, and spices. Fresh vegetables and fruits were available only in season, although such exotics as oranges, lemons, and grapes (from Spain and packed in cork) could be had in the winter holiday season. Most women canned vegetables and fruits and made their own preserves, chili sauce, and catsup even though all these commodities could be had in the stores. (Need I say that frozen foods were many years in the future?) As a rule, housewives baked their own bread, or most of it. In our family we used bakery bread, and a good product it was—of real heft and with a crisp brown crust unspoiled by wax paper. Even so, every Saturday morning my mother baked rolls, sweet rolls, pies, and a cake or two. No self-respecting cook would have depended on a commercial bakery for these.

At another place in this book I have dealt with women's dress in 1913. I have no recollection of slit skirts or peek-a-boo waists. It may be that I was not enough interested in women to notice what they wore; more probably the innovations had not yet reached the smaller cities. I do remember very clearly the male attire of the time. In essentials it had changed little for many years. All men wore long underwear, cotton in the summer, woolen in the winter. There were no lightweight summer suits. (I saw my first summer suit in 1925, when I went to live and work in Springfield, Illinois, one of the hotter localities of the country. The suit was a seersucker, which I still believe to be the coolest of summer garments.) Work shirts came with collars attached; dress shirts were made for detachable collars, of linen for the more affluent, of celluloid for those who had to economize. (The celluloid collar could be cleaned at home; the linen collar had to be sent to the laundry.) Haircuts cost a quarter and no tip, shaves fifteen cents. For women there were no beauty shops. In our town, when weddings or other important social events made beauty treatments imperative, a diminutive, respected Negress, America Spencer by name, trotted from house to house to administer them. Boys started to wear long pants when they left grade school—all, that is, except a pitiable few who were so far behind in growth that their parents would not invest in clothes certain to be outgrown soon.

At the approach of winter every owner of an automobile, at least in the North, jacked it up on blocks, drained the radiator, and reconciled himself to the fact that the car would stay in the garage, usually a former stable, until spring. In Mansfield the streets were completely devoid of automobile traffic in the winter. We lived near a long hill, perfect for sledding. For the benefit of the boys of the neighborhood the property owners on one side of the street refrained from shoveling the sidewalks after a snow. More than that, they permitted us, after school, to draw tubs of water with which we iced the trampled walks. In an hour or so we had an ideal surface, icy, fast, but rough enough that sleds could be steered. On Flexible Flyers, on old-fashioned wooden sleds with round steel runners, on a variety of bobsleds, all homemade, we coasted down that hill at speeds between thirty and forty miles an hour. There was no danger whatever of a collision with a vehicle, either horse-drawn or motor, at any of the several cross streets.

Social life was simple: some calling, especially in the summer, a picnic now and then, an occasional church supper or church-sponsored entertainment, and rarely, an evening at the Opera House to see a play or minstrel show by a touring company. There was vaudeville, but respectable people did not patronize it. My parents rarely entertained or visited friends. As a family we attended the annual Sunday School picnic, the annual grocers' picnic (much more fun), and the annual Burton Holmes travel lecture. Sunday School and church were obligatory. There was no parental objection to cards but we never played. Reading, mostly magazines, was our sole diversion. My older sister played the piano and played well, but we had no Victrola. Neither did anyone of my acquaintance.

I wish I could remember where I was when the year came to an end on the night of December 31. Since I had turned thirteen only a week earlier I must have been at home. At 10:30 or thereabouts my father would have been asleep over the *Saturday Evening Post;* my mother, up since 6:30, would have been nodding over her mending. The three young children, a girl and two boys, would have been bedded down for a couple of hours; my older sister was in Dallas, studying music. So I would have gone to the kitchen for the nightly snack: cheese—Herkimer, aged

Wisconsin brick, or imported Swiss (none of your devitalized stuff in packages)—or a saucer-full of raw oysters, supplemented with pie and coffee. And then I would have gone to bed, unaware that I had just passed through a pivotal year, and without the slightest suspicion that I would ever write a book about it.

INDEX

Index

Index

Index

INDEX

Index

Index

INDEX

INDEX

Index

Index

PRINTED IN U.S.A.